WILDFLOWERS OF THE WEST

WILDFLOWERS OF THE WEST

Written and Illustrated by

MABEL CRITTENDEN and DOROTHY TELFER

CELESTIAL ARTS
MILLBRAE, CALIFORNIA

Published by CELESTIAL ARTS, 231 Adrian Road, Millbrae, California 94030

First printing: October, 1975
Manufactured in the United States of America

Library of Congress Cataloging in Publication Data

Crittenden, Mabel,   1917-
   Wildflowers of the West.

   Bibliography: p.
   Includes index.
   1. Wild flowers - - The West - - Identification.
I.   Telfer, Dorothy W., joint author.   II.   Title.
QK133.C74   582'.13'0978   75-9076
ISBN 0-89087-069-1

   2   3   4   5   6   7   8   9   10   —   80   79   78   77   76

CONTENTS

PREFACE

There has long been a need for a book such as this. Every young person in the West looks at the wonderful variety of wildflowers that grow from the seashore to the mountain tops, from the Golden Gate to the crest of the Rockies and from Canada to Mexico and wants to know their names or how to learn their names. Until now, few have had the good fortune to be set on the path leading to the desired knowledge.

The wealth of western wildflowers is so great, numbering several thousand kinds, only an outstanding botanist might be expected to know more than a small fraction of them offhand. Parents and teachers, to whom children go with most of their questions, have had to answer, over and over, "I'm sorry, but I don't know the names of our wildflowers. I wish that I did or that I had some way of learning their names." A few have had courses in systematic botany and have learned how to use keys for identification, but such persons are rare in the public schools, or as parents.

The general feeling of futility in regard to wildflower names no longer has any need for existence. Mabel Crittenden and Dorothy Telfer provide the hitherto lacking route to the desired knowledge. To be sure, this book describes and illustrates only the common wildflowers that are most likely to be found, or the characteristics of the families of flowers that are most frequently encountered. What is more important, though, it acquaints the user with the methods through which the literature on wildflowers can be made to yield the identity of any flower that may be encountered, or the family to which it belongs. In a manner so clear and simple that it can be learned by any boy or girl, or by any adult, this book introduces the user to the techniques of plant identification by means of a "key" that are employed by professional botanists.

During the past several years, Mrs. Crittenden and Mrs. Telfer have successfully shown the boys and girls of grades 3 to 5 in the Corte Madera School, of the Portola Valley School District, how to identify wildflowers by the very methods that are presented in this book. The response of the young people has been enthusiastic to the point that flower identification has become one of their favorite studies. The content of the book is, therefore, already "tried and true." In addition the children have also learned the basic reasons for the use of technical names and something of what is meant by "plant families." They have become fairly well versed in the elements of "systematic botany."

From this point onward, the extent of an individual's learning will be determined only by his ambition and desire for further knowledge. Gratifyingly, the information and methodology that have been learned are of a type that never will be forgotten. At any desired time later in life, the study of plant identification can be resumed with complete success. A teacher, though helpful, no longer will be needed.

This book is assured of complete success anywhere there are wildflowers to identify. From the wonderworld it opens up, the student can go on to increasingly more difficult and more technical books to aid him in identifying the many kinds of wildflowers that cannot be included in an introductory book such as this one. And always, the seeker will be rewarded by the satisfaction that comes from real accomplishments.

Carl D. Duncan, Ph.D.
San Jose State University

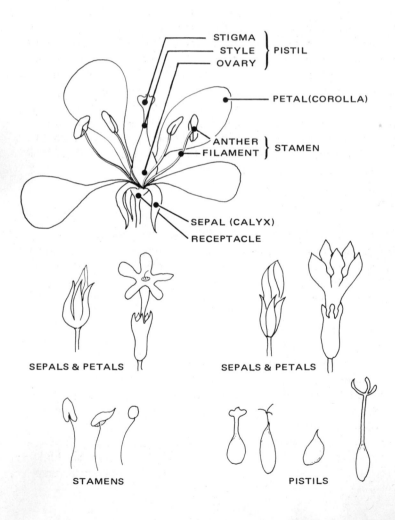

STIGMA ⎫
STYLE ⎬ PISTIL
OVARY ⎭

PETAL(COROLLA)

ANTHER   ⎫
FILAMENT ⎬ STAMEN

SEPAL (CALYX)
RECEPTACLE

SEPALS & PETALS

SEPALS & PETALS

STAMENS

PISTILS

Chapter I

CLUES TO FLOWER
IDENTIFICATION

Flower Parts

1. *SEPALS* The outermost circle of parts are the *sepals*. While the flower is in the bud stage, the sepals are wrapped around all the other parts to protect them. In a few flowers, the sepals are pushed off when the bud opens. In others, they turn downward under the open petals. In some, they stay on and surround the growing ovary. In a few flowers, the sepals remain on the plant long after the petals drop and the seeds are scattered.

In most flowers, the sepals are green, but they may be brightly colored and look so much like petals that it is easy to confuse them. This is true of many Lilies and Irises, but though colored alike, they are arranged in two circles. The outer ones are the sepals, the inner ones the petals. Thus, Lilies have three sepals and three petals, not six petals, as they seem to have.

If the flower has only one circle of petal-like parts, botanists speak of them as sepals, even if they are brightly colored and look like petals. All the sepals together are called the *calyx*. This term is used most frequently when the sepals are united. Count the tips to determine the number of fused sepals.

2. *PETALS* Inside the sepals are the *petals*, the colorful, attractive part of the flower. All petals together are the *corolla*, sometimes united into a *corolla tube*. Count the petal lobes to know the number of fused petals. Petals vary in shape and number in different types of flowers. They may be all alike or an irregular vase-shaped corolla with upper and lower lips, like a snapdragon. The petals usually fade and drop after the seeds begin to develop. A few flowers have no petals. The number of petals and whether or not they are united is so basic that the chapters of this book are arranged on that basis.

3. *STAMENS*   The *stamens* form the third circle. Often they are the yellow, fuzzy part in the flower center, but they may be any color and vary in number, depending on the flower group. A few flowers have no stamens. The stamens are the male organs which produce the pollen used to fertilize the ovules of the flower. Pollen is a powder made up of very tiny grains, or spores, which comes out of the little bag, or sac, at the tip of the stamen called the *anther,* held at the end of a slender stalk called the *filament.* Sometimes the filaments are united in a collar around the *pistil.*

4. *PISTIL*   The *pistil* is the female organ, the seed-producing part of the flower. It is made up of three parts: (1) The top is the *stigma* which catches the pollen; it may open into furry or sticky branches when it is mature. (2) the *style* connects the stigma to the third part of the pistil; it holds the stigma at the right height to fit the needs of that flower; not every flower has a style. (3) The *ovary* is the enlarged base of the pistil; it is a bag holding the *ovules* which are the future seeds. A *superior ovary* is up inside the blossom, with petals, sepals, and stamens attached below it. If the ovary is below where the petals are attached, it is called an *inferior ovary.* Usually you can see the inferior ovary by looking at the back or underside of the flower. To see a superior ovary, you must look into the flower. This is especially true if the petals or sepals are united.

After the ovules are fertilized, they develop into seeds. As the seeds grow, the ovary grows larger and develops the *fruit,* which is the mature ovary, containing mature seeds. A flower may have one, two, or many pistils, which may be simple, with one ovule, or compound, made of many united sections and developing several ovules. The number of pistils generally matches the number of petals.

Other Clues to Help Identify Flowers

1. The *receptacle* is the enlarged end of the flower stem in which the flower sits. It usually appears to be a continuation of the stem.

2. The *bracts* are not found on all flowers. They are specialized leaves which may look like sepals or petals. They often are brightly colored, but they enclose a *group* of flowers—sepals enclose just one flower. The red "petals" of poinsetta are bracts. The individual flowers of these plants are very tiny and not easily noticed, but they contain the necessary parts, the pistils and stamens, so are the true flowers of the plant.

3. *Specialized Arrangements*   In the huge Sunflower or Composite Family, the blossoms are made up of *many* tiny flowers, surrounded by bracts. These modified leaves form an involucre around the tightly clustered flowers. It is as though someone had taken a stem of flowers and pushed them all up to the top into a tight head, surrounded by some of the leaves which also were pushed up. In flowers like daisies and sunflowers, the center might *seem* to be the stamens. Look closely and see that these are tiny flowers all packed together, each having petals, stamens and pistil. Pull a head carefully apart. These center flowers are called *disc flowers*. Each has a corolla of five tiny petals, united into a tiny tube, with just the tips free. There are five stamens held in tightly by the petals. The simple pistil has an inferior ovary, with a slender style, and a stigma which opens into two branches to catch the pollen. The calyx is very reduced and in many plants of this family is merely made of hairs or fuzz like the dandelion fuzz which is seen in the fluffy seed head.

In daisies, the disc flowers are surrounded by "petals"; really they are tiny modified one-sided flowers. These are called *ray* flowers, and have been developed to advertise the disc flowers so all will be pollinated by insects. They may have just stamens or just pistils or neither. Some ray flowers show three to five petal lobes separated by notches at the tips.

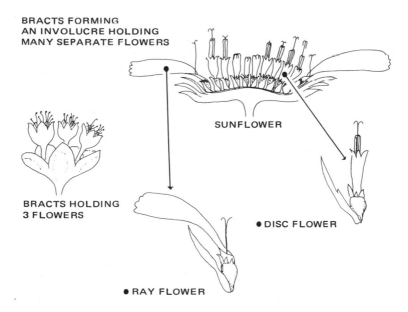

BRACTS FORMING
AN INVOLUCRE HOLDING
MANY SEPARATE FLOWERS

SUNFLOWER

BRACTS HOLDING
3 FLOWERS

● DISC FLOWER

● RAY FLOWER

In flowers, the arrangement might be: *solitary,* with just one blossom at the end of a branch (as poppy); an *umbel,* with many small flowers grouped together at the same height (wild carrot), more or less flat across the top; a *head* with many flowers growing together in a rounded arrangement; a *spike* and a *raceme* have several flowers growing along the branch.

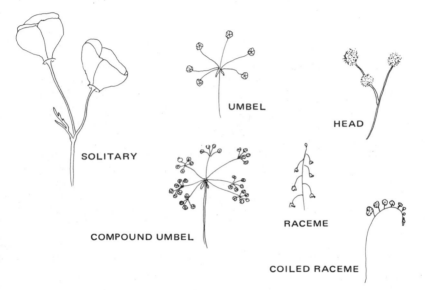

4. *Habitat* is the kind of home in which the flower grows best, as woods or sunny fields, etc. This may be still another clue to identification. In describing each flower, we have given its habitat.

5. *Kind of fruit* is often a clue to identification. A fruit is anything that holds the ripened seeds of the plants—not just something we eat. Often the fruits of wildflowers scarcely can be seen covering the ripe seeds. The fruit is formed from the ovary, sometimes with other parts included, as the receptacle in apples and berries. Some fruits are berries, some are dry capsules or pods. Some have a single hard seed, like plums; some are small and hard with one seed inside, like a sunflower. Some, like dandelion and thistle, have silky ''parachutes'' to carry them; some have burrs or hooks to help them get carried. Every ovary will mature into fruit if even one of its ovules is fertilized; the ovule develops into a seed and the ovary becomes the fruit, or container of the seed.

KINDS OF FRUIT

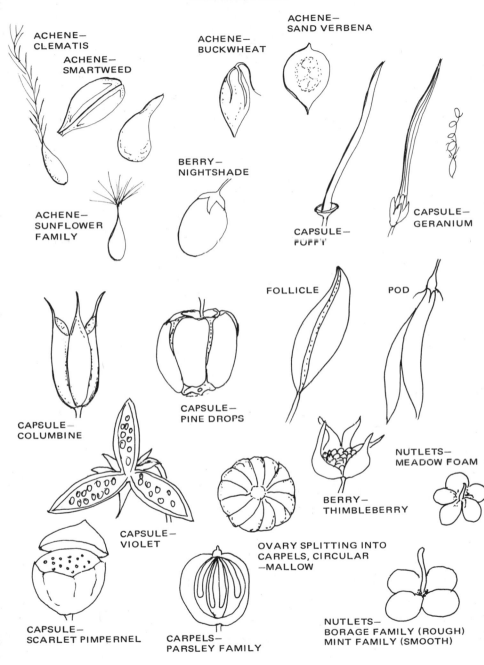

ACHENE—
CLEMATIS

ACHENE—
SMARTWEED

ACHENE—
BUCKWHEAT

ACHENE—
SAND VERBENA

BERRY—
NIGHTSHADE

ACHENE—
SUNFLOWER
FAMILY

CAPSULE—
POPPY

CAPSULE—
GERANIUM

FOLLICLE

POD

CAPSULE—
COLUMBINE

CAPSULE—
PINE DROPS

NUTLETS—
MEADOW FOAM

BERRY—
THIMBLEBERRY

CAPSULE—
VIOLET

OVARY SPLITTING INTO
CARPELS, CIRCULAR
—MALLOW

CAPSULE—
SCARLET PIMPERNEL

CARPELS—
PARSLEY FAMILY

NUTLETS—
BORAGE FAMILY (ROUGH)
MINT FAMILY (SMOOTH)

LEAF SHAPES

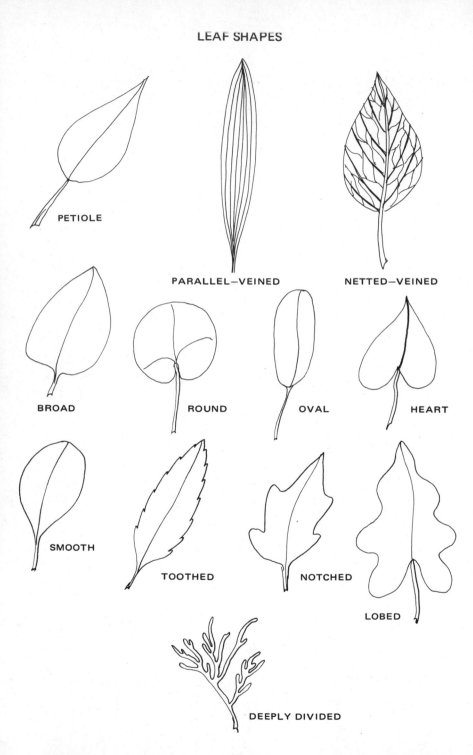

PETIOLE

PARALLEL—VEINED

NETTED—VEINED

BROAD

ROUND

OVAL

HEART

SMOOTH

TOOTHED

NOTCHED

LOBED

DEEPLY DIVIDED

6. *Leaves* may help distinguish flower families or similar flowers from each other. The expanded part of the leaf is called the *blade;* the *petiole* is the stalk which attaches it to the plant. Usually leaves in which the blade is long and narrow have veins that run parallel to the leaf edge. These are called *parallel-veined* leaves, and are typical of Lily, Iris and Grass Families. If the veins form a network in the blade, we call the leaf *netted-veined.* Most plants have this type of veins.

The blade of netted-veined leaves may be many shapes: broad, round, oval, heart-shaped, etc. The margin of the blade may be smooth, toothed, notched, lobed, etc. It may be deeply divided (as in a poppy leaf). There are two ways veins can be arranged: *pinnately* (as a feather) with side veins branching all along· the main vein; *palmately* with several veins radiating from one point (as fingers from the palm of your hand). Deeply lobed leaves are often palmately veined.

Leaves are *simple* when there is only one blade. The leaf is called *compound* when the blade is divided clear to the midrib, making several leaflets on the same petiole. There are two kinds of compound leaves: *pinnately compound,* when leaflets are arranged along the length of the petiole (roses); *palmately compound,* if leaflets are arranged radiating from the end of the petiole (lupine, clover).

The way leaves are arranged on the plant is often a clue for identification. On some plants the leaves grow directly from the crown of the roots, around the base of the flower stalk (as in most evening primroses). These are called *basal* leaves, forming a *rosette*. On most plants, the leaves grow along the branches. If only one leaf grows at a place with leaves alternating up the branch, they are called *alternate*. If two grow at one place, one on each side of the branch, they are called *opposite*. If several grow at one place, all around the stem, they are called *whorled*. If the leaves seem to sit right on the stem, they are called sessile.

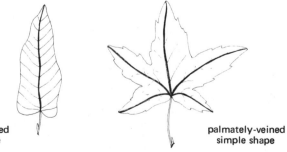

pinnately-veined
simple shape

palmately-veined
simple shape

LEAF SHAPES

LEAF ARRANGEMENTS

pinnately-compound

palmately-compound leaf

opposite leaf arrangement

alternate leaf arrangement

whorled leaf arrangement

Chapter II

FOLLOWING THE CLUES

Follow the Clues of the Tabs

Notice the printed tabs that appear on the right side of the following pages. These tabs give clues for finding your flowers with their descriptions and pictures. Flowers with three petals are described and pictured on pages with three printed tabs. If your flower has four, look on the pages with the same number of tabs (four) as there are petals. If the petals grow together at the base, or are "united," the tabs are united, so look on those pages. There you will find pictures to match your flower, and many interesting facts about it. So, count your petals and look for the same number of tabs.

OR

Follow the Clues of the Botanical Key

Carefully inspect your flower. Find the petals and sepals. Count them. Are they fused or separate? How many stamens and pistils are there? Where is the ovary lcoated? Look at both buds and open flowers to find all parts; look at more than one flower. Look at the leaves.

NOW: Look at the *KEY* that begins on page 11. The clues are in words and pictures and are arranged in pairs or triplets. Your flower will fit one of the first pair. Does it fit clue 1-a or 1-b? When you are sure, follow the directions the clue gives you.

Let's use the *KEY* to identify a common yellow mustard. How many petals, sepals, stamens, and pistils has it? It has four petals, four sepals, six stamens, and one pistil. Four of the stamens are long and two are short.

1a. {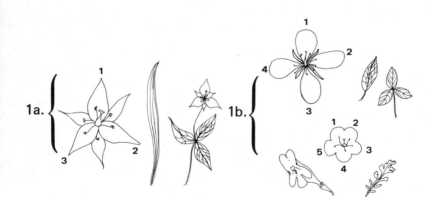

1b. {

1c. {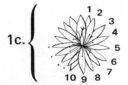

Look at the *KEY*. See the picture on the page facing each clue. First, look at clue 1-a. The mustard has four petals, not three, as in this clue, so 1-a does not fit. Look at 1-b. This does fit; do as the *KEY* says and go on to clue 3. Look at 3-a. This clue does not fit mustard, because mustard has both petals and sepals, so you must choose the other clue, 3-b. This tells you to go on to clue 6.

Clue 6-a fits, because the petals are separate, not joined—see the illustration on the facing page to note the difference. Go on to clue 7 as directed. Clue 7 asks about the number of stamens. Mustard has less than ten, so fits 7-b; go on to 11. The ovary is superior, as in 11-a, so go to clue 12 as the *KEY* directs. The petals are all alike, only 12-b fits, so go on to clue 14. Clue 14-a is correct because there are four petals, four sepals, and six stamens. Go to clue 15 where you will find that the flower belongs to the Mustard Family and tells you where to find the illustrations and descriptions of the most common members of this family.

After you have practiced using the *KEY* a few times, you will become expert with it and can find the family of the common Western wildflowers. However, you *must* remember the circles, so you can distinguish between petals and sepals, and when keying flowers in heads, you *must* be sure to take the head apart so you are looking at *only one flower*. This is especially true of the Composite Family which has many tiny flowers tightly grouped together and surrounded by leafy bracts. They seem to have many *petals;* really, they have many *flowers*.

The Key

Carefully examine one flower. Count the sepals, petals, stamens, pistils; open a flower or cut it in half if you need to.

1

a.   If all flower parts are in threes (there may seem to be six, but never four or five), and all leaves are parallel-veined or grass-like (except Trillium) . . .go to clue 2

b.   If the flower parts are in fours or fives but not in threes, and if the leaves are netted-veined, simple or divided . . .   go to clue 3

c.   If each flower has more than five true petals . . .turn to page 161

2a. {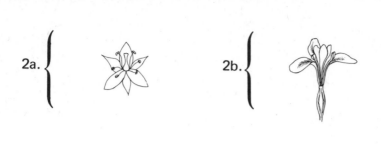

2b. {

3a. {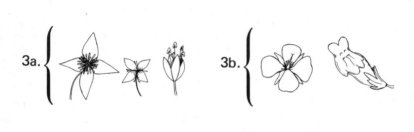

3b. {

4a. {

4b. {

5a. {

5b. {

2

a. If the ovary is superior (above attachment of calyx and corolla—you may have to open flower), it is in the Lily Family . . .   turn to page 41

b. If the ovary is inferior (below the base of the other flower parts), it is in the Iris Family . . . turn to page 53

3

a. If the flowers have sepals but no petals (calyx may be colored and appear petal-like, but there will be only one "circle" of "petals," not two circles as when you have both petals and sepals) . . .   go to clue 4

b. If flowers have both petals and sepals (sepals of poppies fall off as the flower opens, so look at buds and flowers) . . .   go to clue 6

4

a. If sepals are united into a tubular calyx which may be colored and look like petals, with leaves opposite, it is in the Four O'Clock Family . . .   turn to page 35

b. If sepals are not united, are colored and appear petal-like, or are greenish, yellowish, or dry . . .   go to clue 5

5

a. Calyx of five or six parts, yellowish, greenish, or reddish, drying persistent, one-celled superior ovary, four to nine stamens—it is in the Buckwheat Family . . .   turn to page 31

b. Calyx of four or five parts, often petal-like or colored, surrounding many one-celled simple pistils clustered on a mound; many stamens—it is anemone or clematis in the Buttercup Family . . .   turn to pages 37, 38

6a. {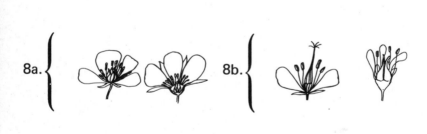

6b. {

7a. {

7b. {

8a. {

8b. {

9a. {

9b. {

14

6

a. If petals are separate from each other, not joined (lower two petals in pea-shaped flowers seem lightly joined, shaped like a boat keel) . . .   go to clue 7

b. If all petals are joined to each other, at least at the base . . .   go to clue 26

7

a. More than ten stamens (more than double the number of petals) . . .   go to clue 8

b. Ten stamens or less . . .   go to clue 11

8

a. Two or more ovaries clustered together but each separate (sometimes grouped atop a small central mound or enclosed in calyx cup) . . .   go to clue 9

b. One ovary; may be compound ovary with one to many styles or stigmas (Saxifrage ovaries may be only lightly joined) . . .   go to clue 10

9

a. Stamens attached to receptacle below pistils and not attached to calyx; simple separate superior ovaries on a small central mound—the Buttercup Family(if the corolla is irregular, see larkspur and monkshood pp. 75, 117) . . .   turn to page 81

b. Stamens attached to calyx or to a disc or rim that lines calyx tube or cup; ovaries often partly or completely enclosed by calyx tube; tiny pair of leaf-like structures (stipules) at base of leaves, leaves usually compound—the Rose Family . . .   turn to page 89

10a. {  10b. {

11a. { 11b. {

12a. { 12b. {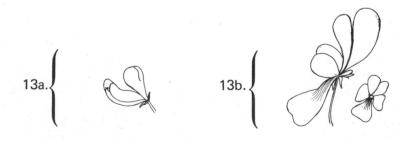

13a. { 13b. {

10

a.   Calyx falls as corolla opens; stamens attached to the base of petals, but not to each other—the Poppy Family . . .   turn to page 57

b.   Calyx remaining after corolla opens; stamens united or not . . .   go to clue 11

11

a.   Superior ovary . . .   go to clue 12

b.   Inferior ovary   go to clue 24

12

a.   Petals not all the same shape, corolla irregular   go to clue 13

b.   Petals all the same shape (or almost) . . .   go to clue 14

13

a.   Corolla somewhat like that of sweet peas (one large upper petal which may be folded over others, two side petals, two lightly joined petals shaped like a boat keel)—the Pea Family . . .   turn to page 109

b.   Corolla like pansies or violets (two upright petals, two side petals, one lower petal with a spur)—the Violet Family . . .   turn to page 115

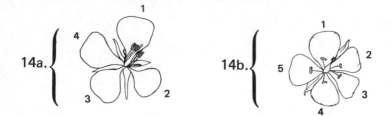

14a. {

14b. {

15a. {

15b. {

16a. {

16b. {

17a. {

17b. {

17c.

14

a. Four petals, four sepals, six stamens . . .   go to clue 15

b. Five petals . . .   go to clue 16

15

a. Six stamens (usually having four long, two short); simple leaves, sometimes divided, but not compound; petals with claws (usually) and arranged in the form of a cross—the Mustard Family . . .   turn to page 59

b. Stamens not with one pair short; leaves palmately compound, usually with three leaflets—the Caper Family . . .   turn to page 63

16

a. Leaves like clover, palmately compound—the Oxalis Family . . .   turn to page 95

b. Leaves not palmately compound . . .   go to clue 17

17

a. Two sepals (usually), five stamens (usually), three styles (usually); flower withers quickly—the Purslane Family . . .   turn to page 79

b. Four or five sepals, sometimes joined into a tube, stamens separate . . .   go to clue 18

c. Calyx is five-lobed, often with bracts; stamens numerous with filaments united into a column; petals attached to base of column—the Mallow Family . . .   turn to page 93

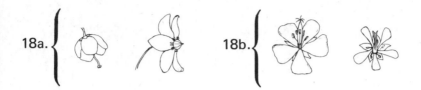

18a. 18b.

  19a.  19b.

20a. 20b.

21a.  21b.

18

a.   One single style . . .   go to clue 19

b.   Two to five separate styles, or joined except at
     tip . . .   go to clue 20

19

a.   Style persistent; compound ovary does not
     break into separate nutlets; simple leaves—the
     Heath Family including the Wintergreen Fam-
     ily . . .   turn to page 105

b.   Style withers early; compound ovary breaks
     into five small nutlets; finely divided leaves
     which are not evergreen—the Meadow Foam
     Family . . .   turn to page 89

20

a.   Five styles (closely joined together), with five
     late-opening stigmas; the styles grow into long
     "beaks" as the pistils mature; compound pistil
     then splits with each style coiling separately;
     five (sometimes ten) stamens; usually pinkish
     or lavender flowers—the Geranium Family
     . . .   turn to page 87

b.   Two to five styles which do not form long
     "beaks" and which remain attached to ovary
     . . .   go to clue 21

21

a.   Opposite leaves along stems . . .   go to clue 22

b.   Alternate or basal leaves . . .   to to clue 23

22a.

22b.

23a.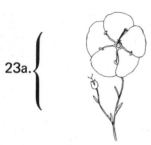

23b.

24a.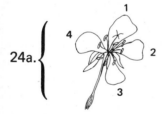

1
4
2
3

24b.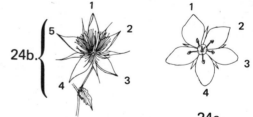

5
1
2
3
4

24c.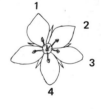

1
2
3
4

25a.

25b.

22

22

a. Many stamens, often in two or three groups, one- to three-celled ovary with three styles; leaves and branches opposite—the St. John's Wort Family . . . turn to page 95

b. Stamens the same number or double that of petals; five (or four) sepals, sometimes joined into a tube; one-celled ovary with two or three styles; leaves opposite—the Pink Family . . . turn to page 99

23

a. Five stamens slightly fused at base; compound ovary; petals fall very early; mostly blue-flowered—the Flax Family . . . turn to page 97

b. Stamens separate, same number (or double the number) of petals; ovaries sometimes only lightly fused; flowers usually white, sometimes red, never blue; leaves usually basal—the Saxifrage Family . . . turn to page 85

24

a. Four petals, four calyx lobes, eight stamens-—the Evening Primrose Family . . . turn to page 65

b. Five (or ten) petals, five sepals, numerous stamens; rough, hairy plants or small bushes—the Loasa Family . . . turn to page 101

c. Five petals, five sepals (fused and often tiny), five to ten stamens . . . go to clue 25

25

a. Flowers very small, either in flat umbels or gathered into small balls; five stamens—the Parsley Family . . . turn to page 103

b. Flowers small but not in umbels or balls; two to five styles or stigmas; five-lobed calyx; five to ten stamens—the Saxifrage Family . . . turn to page 85

26a. {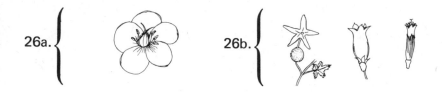

26b. {

27a. {

27b. {

28a. {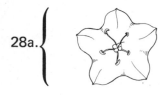

28b. {

29a. {

29b. {

26
  a. Superior ovary . . .   go to clue 27

  b. Inferior ovary . . .   go to clue 37

27
  a. Five stamens or less, attached to corolla (open flower if necessary) . . .   go to clue 28

  b. Five or ten stamens, not attached to corolla—the Heath Family . . .   turn to page 121

28
  a. Corolla lobes all alike (flower regular) . . .   go to clue 29

  b. Corolla appears two-lipped, or at least not all lobes are shaped alike . . .   go to clue 36

29
  a. Stamens stand in front of each lobe or corolla; stamens same number as corolla lobes; one style—the Primrose Family . . .   turn to page 127

  b. Each of the stamens alternate with lobes of corolla; stamens are the same number or fewer than corolla lobes . . .   go to clue 30

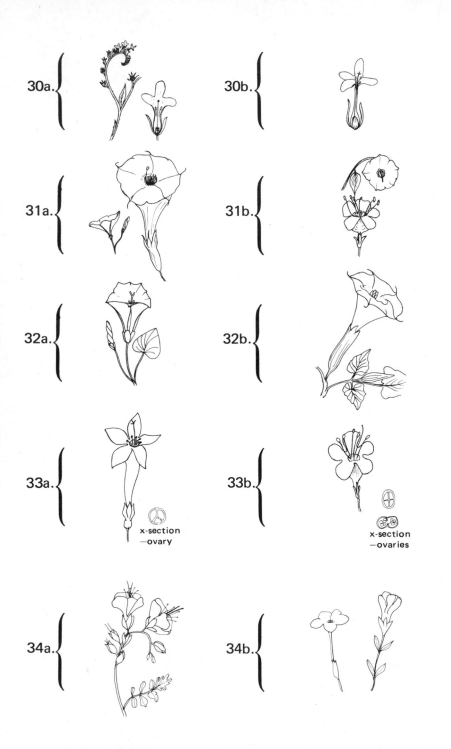

30a. {

30b. {

31a. {

31b. {

32a. {

32b. {

33a. {

x-section
—ovary

33b. {

x-section
—ovaries

34a. {

34b. {

30
a. Ovary distinctly four-lobed on outside; one style; flowers in coils which unroll as flower opens—the Borage Family . . .   turn to page 137

b. Ovary compound but not four-lobed on outside   go to clue 31

31
a. Flowers large and funnel-shaped (like morning glories) . . .   go to clue 32

b. Flowers small (not like morning glories) . . .   go to clue 33

32
a. One style, two stigmas, petals twisted in bud, sepals not joined—Convolvulus in the Morning Glory Family . . .   turn to page 129

b. One style, one stigma (two-lobed), sepals joined into a tube—Datura in the Nightshade Family . . .   turn to page 143

33
a. Style with three stigmas (examine several flowers to be sure stigmas are mature enough to be open); three-celled ovary, five petals, five sepals, five stamens—the Gilia or Phlox Family . . .   turn to page 131

b. Style not three-parted, one- or two-celled ovary . . .   go to clue 34

34
a. Five sepals, separate (or almost); two styles (or two stigmas); long stamens; flowers often in coils which unroll as they bloom—the Phacelia Family . . .   turn to page 133

b. Sepals completely joined except at tip; one style . . .   go to clue 35

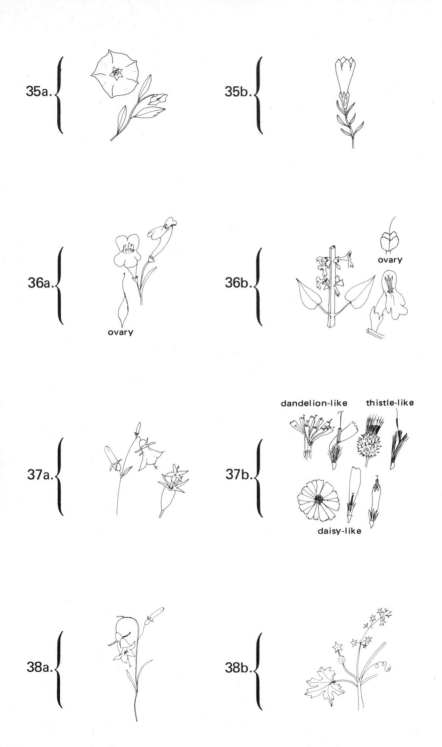

35a.

35b.

36a.

ovary

36b.

ovary

37a.

37b.

dandelion-like   thistle-like

daisy-like

38a.

38b.

35
a. One style with one stigma; two-celled ovary; corolla with very shallow lobes; leaves alternate—the Nightshade Family . . .   turn to page 141

b. One-celled ovary, four- or five-lobed corolla, leaves opposite—the Gentian Family . . .   turn to page 125

36
a. Two-lipped corolla; ovary not four-lobed on outside; stem not square; four stamens with anthers (or two with anthers), fifth stamen (with no anther) sometimes present; stamens stand in pairs; usually very colorful flowers- —the Figwort Family . . .   turn to page 149

b. Two-lipped corolla; four-lobed ovary; leaves with mint odor; two or four stamens; square stem—the Mint Family . . .   turn to page 145

37
a. Flowers separate (not in heads) . . .   go to clue 38

b. Individual flowers small, but are tightly gathered into a head, held by a calyx-like cup of bracts; flowers look like sunflowers, daisies, dandelions, or thistles—the Composite Family . . .   turn to page 167

38
a. Small bell-like flowers (usually blue); stamens and pistils in same flower—the Bellflower or Campanula Family . . .   turn to page 139

b. Trumpet-shaped or flaring imperfect flowers (large and yellow, or small and white) on trailing or climbing plants; pistillate flower has a noticeable round inferior ovary—the Gourd Family . . .   turn to page 119

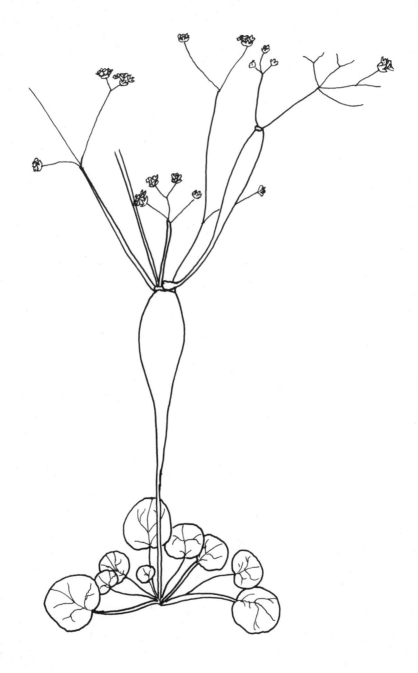

Chapter III

FLOWERS WITH SEPALS
BUT NO PETALS

Strange as it may seem, some flowers have no petals at all. In many of these flowers the calyx looks like the corolla and has divisions that look like petals. Sometimes they are colored like petals. In using this book to identify flowers, it is important to examine flowers carefully to make sure whether there are petals or sepals, or both. If there is only one "circle" they are sepals.

BUCKWHEAT FAMILY
Polygonaceae

The Buckwheat Family has many members growing in most parts of the West, from sea level to high mountains. They often are the most noticeable plants to be seen on the shrubby hills of the West. In the spring, their feathery white or yellow blossoms are tinged with pink. In late summer the bloosoms turn to rusty red fruits, still very decorative. Most of the plants are annual, and may look woody at the base. The small flowers usually grow in umbels, and have no petals. The calyx is white or pinkish, or yellow, and usually is divided into five or six parts. Stamens vary in number from three to nine, partly attached to the calyx. The ovary is superior, one-celled, and often triangular in shape, with two or three styles. Buckwheats have a cup-shaped circle of bracts surrounding the flower cluster. The fruit usually is a triangular, one-seeded achene which looks like grain. It may be brown, gray, or black. The dry umbels of fruits keep for many weeks when cut, so often are included in dry flower arrangements.

The leaves are simple, often hairy, and most of the species form a thick cluster or rosette around the base of the stems. Those leaves that grow on the stems are smaller and alternate. Most Buckwheat grows to be 1-3 feet (30-90 cm) high. Usually they are found at any altitude, on the drier, rockier, or warmer slopes.

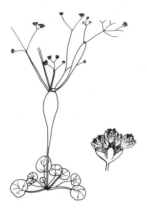

DESERT BUCKWHEAT

SULFUR FLOWER

MOUNTAIN SORREL

SHEEP SORREL

flower   seed

CURLY DOCK

32

Many of the species are among the plants commonly called "weeds," such as dock, sheep sorrel, and knotweed. Other species are domestically grown in northern Asia, Europe and America and used to make buckwheat flour. The Buckwheats produce a great deal of nectar so are important plants for bees. Princess plume, heart's ease, and rhubarb are members of this family which are grown in gardens all over the world.

Desert Buckwheat, Indian Pipe, Desert Trumpet, Bottle Plant, *Eriogonum inflatum,* is a many-branched plant, ½-3 feet tall, with heart-shaped basal leaves. Just above the rossette of leaves the stems become inflated, something like long balloons. Above the "balloons" there are many branches, so the upper part seems delicate and net-like, with three to seven small yellowish flowers on each small branch. This plant grows in the deserts of Utah, Arizona, New Mexico, and California. It is abundant at the Grand Canyon, and blooms from spring to fall.

Sulfur Flower, *Eriogonum umbellatum,* has sulfur-yellow, tiny blossoms which hang downwards. The many blossoms are grouped inside an eight-lobed bract and covered with fine fuzz. It grows 3-5 inches (7.5-12.5 cm) high, often coloring a whole slope with its sulfur yellow color. This is a showy plant, the flowers turning orange-copper both in bloom and in seed head as they mature. It grows at 4,000-9,000 feet elevation all over the West.

Mountain Sorrel, *Oxyria digyna,* is a common alpine flower, growing from 4,000-12,000 feet elevation. It is found in meadows and rock slide areas above timberline or along streams at lower altitudes. It has long-stalked, kidney-shaped leaves and bright rose-colored mature fruit. The flowers are small and greenish with specks of red. It is a favorite food for sheep, grouse, elk, and bear. The young leaves are good in salads. It is found worldwide from arctic regions southward.

Sheep Sorrel, *Rumex acetosella,* is low-growing, a dainty, tiny-flowered plant with two kinds of flower stalks. The yellowish stalks have only stamens, the reddish-flowered stalks produce the pistils. After the pollen is shed, the yellowish stalks shrivel, while the developing wings on the sepals of the reddish flower stalks make them more noticeable. Sorrel is excellent food for grazing animals; the leaves have been used for tanning leather; bits of leaves useful to flavor fish and rice. Sorrel is found all over the West; naturalized from Europe.

Curly Dock, *Rumex crispus,* is tall-growing, especially noticeable when the brown-red, enlarged sepals have become winged. The fleshy root once was valued as a tonic; young tender leaves can be cooked like spinach; rich in vitamin A. A very common weed in valleys and up to 4,500 feet in the mountains all over the United States; naturalized from Europe.

PINK SAND VERBENA

YELLOW SAND VERBENA

FOUR O'CLOCK FAMILY
Nyctaginaceae

The Four O'Clocks of the West are juicy herbs with opposite leaves, usually with swollen joints. There are no petals, but the fragile calyx is brightly colored and many flowers are arranged in an umbel with bracts at the base. These bracts may resemble a calyx, but they surround a *group* of flowers rather than just one flower, so are not sepals. The bracts also may be colored. In the bud stage, the true calyx is pleated or folded. It has five (or four) lobes joined into a tube at the base. This persistent base folds tightly over the superior, one-celled ovary, but is not attached to it. There is one style and one stigma. The fruit is an achene which ripens into a very hard, ridged or winged case. The five stamens (sometimes three to seven) are attached to the calyx funnel and are of different lengths. Certain Four O'Clocks are favorites in flower gardens.

Pink Sand Verbena, *Abronia villosa,* is a small, creeping, sandy-area plant, with small bright pink-purple flower umbels so thick they often completely cover the plant. The calyx is flaring and funnel-shaped and is the brightly colored part of this flower. There are many bracts at the base of the umbel. The five stamens are short and are not noticeable. The calyx base persists and becomes winged around the seed-like fruit. Leaves and stems are very hairy. Verbena blooms after the rains come, usually between January and April, sometimes again in September. It is found in southern California deserts, Arizona and Utah, often forming masses of color.

Yellow Sand Verbena, *Abronia latifolia,* has fragrant yellow flowers and very succulent stems and leaves which are almost round. *Abronia maritima* has dark red flowers, and grows on southern California beaches.

Common Seashore Verbena, *Abronia latifolia,* has fragrant yellow flowers and very succulent stems and leaves which are almost round. *Abronia maritima* has dark red flowers, and grows on southern California beaches.

Sand verbenas are native to America. The true verbena, grown as garden flowers, is in the Verbena Family and has both sepals and petals. The family is small with only a few wild species.

CHAPARRAL VIRGIN'S BOWER

WESTERN VIRGIN'S BOWER

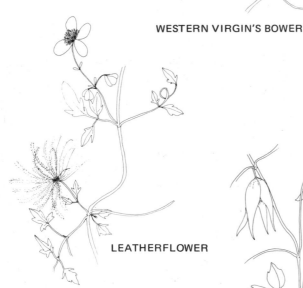

LEATHERFLOWER

BELLRUE

BUTTERCUP FAMILY
Ranunculaceae

Most members of the Buttercup Family have five petals, but the number of petals vary and clematis has no petals at all. The sepals in clematis are petal-like and are often brightly colored, especially in the cultivated species. Most of the wild species have white or creamy sepals, but a few have purplish or brownish sepals. The leaves are opposite on half-woody vines, the only member of this family with these characteristics. Some flowers may have many stamens and no pistils, while other flowers have the pistils and no stamens. A common name applied to many is virgin's bower.

Chaparral Virgin's Bower, Pipe-stem, *Clematis lasiantha*   The blossoms with stamens are more attractive than the pistillate flowers because of the burst of yellow stamens, but all flowers are large and lovely, sometimes more than 2 inches (5 cm) across, creamy to white. This species has only a few flowers in each cluster. The fruit is even more interesting than the blossoms. The many pistils form a cluster of achenes, each one developing a long hairy or feathery tail about 2 inches (5 cm) long. These form large, conspicuous heads which remain on the plant long into the fall or even into the winter. The vines are woody below and grow long enough to climb up, over, and through shrubs and trees on hillsides, 100-2,000 feet elevation all over California. The petioles of the leaves help support the plant, acting as tendrils, twisting around anything the plant climbs over.

Yerba de Chivato, Western Virgin's Bower, *Clematis ligusticifolia*   This Clematis is very similar to chaparral virgin's bower except the blossoms are smaller and grow in bigger clusters; they may be so thick on the vine they nearly cover it. The seed head, however, is not as crowded so the ball is not as big and fuzzy. The juice from this was used by Spanish Californians as a basis for medicine to wash cuts in horses, and by Indians for sore throats and colds. It grows along stream banks and brushlands of hills and mountain, British Columbia to California, east to the Rockies, North Dakota and New Mexico.

Leatherflower, *Clematis drummondii*   This desert clematis forms vines 6-8 feet (1.8-2.4 m) long. The sepals are brownish or brownish-purple with two or three flowers to a stalk. The fruit heads form long feathery tails. It can be found in California, Arizona, and Texas.

Columbia Clematis, Bellrue, *Clematis columbiana*   This clematis, with its lavender-blue, petal-like sepals, resembles garden species closely. It grows in woods and thickets from Alberta and British Columbia south to Oregon, Utah, and Colorado, from valleys to 8,500 feet. The flowers are 2-3 inches (5-7.5 cm) broad, sometimes hanging and bell-like, the sepals long and tapered. They tend to grow singly, one to a leaf axil. The styles become feathery, making the typical fuzzy head.

WESTERN ANEMONE

PASQUE FLOWER

MARSH MARIGOLD

Western Anemone, *Anemone occidentalis,* is a very beautiful flower. The western species grow high in the mountains, 3,000-9,000 feet in open, wooded areas, flats or valleys. They are among the first flowers to bloom in the spring, sometimes closely following the snowbanks.

There are several species, varying slightly from one to another. Most of them grow about a foot (30 cm) tall on thick woolly stems, usually with only one blossom at the tip. The basal leaves are divided, and those on the stems are so finely divided that they appear feathery. The five creamy yellow sepals form a flower about 2 inches (5 cm) across. They are slightly hairy on the outside and sometimes appear tinged with blue or purple. There are many yellow stamens and several one-celled pistils, all combined in a golden center. The seed heads are nearly as lovely as the flower, forming large fluffy balls. Grows in the Coast Ranges and Sierra Nevada from central California through Oregon and Washington north to British Columbia and east to the Rocky Mountains.

Pasque Flower, *Anemone patens,* is a lovely purple or lavender (rarely white), cup-shaped flower resembling western anemone. It also has very divided leaves and hairy stems. Each flower blooms at the top of a 2-14 inch (5-35 cm) stem with several mostly naked stems growing from a branched root crown. Blooms in very early spring; then the flower stem lengthens and the persistent long feathery styles make a lovely noticeable fuzzy seed head. Grows in moist meadows and woods at 4,000-9,000 feet from Alaska south into the Northwest, then south and east to Illinois and Texas.

Marsh Marigold, Cowslip, Anemone, *Caltha leptosepala*   A dazzling white high-mountain, marshy-meadow and stream-bank flower. The large white buttercup-like flowers have bright clusters of many yellow stamens surrounding the mound of simple pistils. There are no petals; the six to nine sepals are petal-like, forming a flower 1-2 inches (2.5-5 cm) across. Often they are bluish on the underside. Marsh marigolds are among the first flowers to bloom in the mountains, appearing at the edge of melting snowbanks, following spring up the mountainside. The round basal leaves grow from a perennial rootstalk; they are bright green and quite thick, often showing purple veins on the underside.

This water-loving plant is found blooming in or beside icy cold streams and carpeting marshy meadows in the high mountain areas of the West from Alaska to British Columbia, south to California, east to Alberta and south through the Rockies to Arizona and New Mexico; found up to 12,000 feet. The eastern species, *Caltha palustris,* is very similar.

Chapter IV

FLOWERS WITH THREE PETALS
(but may seem to have six)

Most of the flowers that seem to have six petals, have three petals in the inside circle and three sepals in the outside circle which are colored alike, thus masquerading as six petals. All flowers that seem to have six petals, but have parallel-veined leaves, really have three petals and three sepals, not six petals.

LILY FAMILY
Liliaceae

In the Lily Family the three petals and three sepals often are colored and shaped very much alike and may grow upwards like petals. There are six stamens with filaments sometimes quite broad or winged. The stigma may have three bumps. The ovary is three-parted and superior. Flowers may be in umbels. All Lilies grow from bulbs, corms, or rootstocks. Agricultural plants which are members of this family are asparagus and onions. Garden flowers are tiger lily and tulips.

Mariposas *(Calochortus)* are beautiful, showy Lilies with three broad petals which may be white, yellow, lilac, or bluish. They usually have a colored spot near their base. Even if there is no showy spot, there are long hairs and a nectar gland near the base of each petal. The sepals are narrow, sometimes paler than the petals, or greenish, and in the open blossom, grow downwards below the petals. The plant is simply branched with blossoms on the ends of slender stems. The parallel-veined leaves are long and narrow, often withered by the time the flowers bloom. They grow on dry hillsides or shady glens and only in the West. They can be found as far north as Canada, south to Mexico and east to Nebraska. The bulbs were used for food by the Indians.

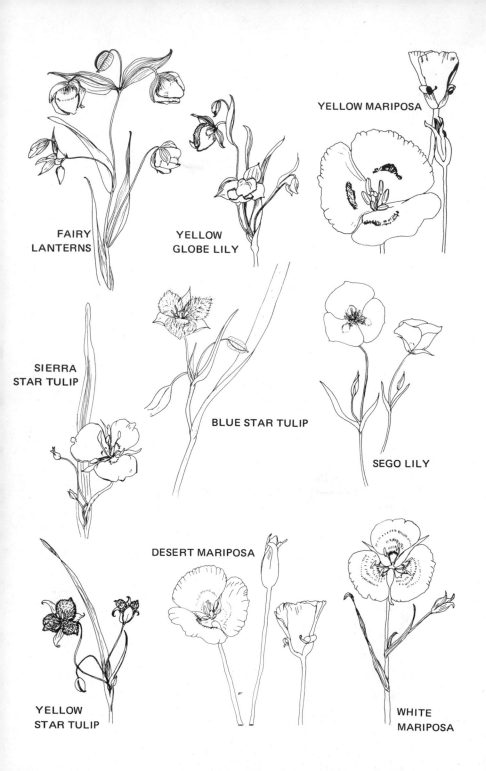

FAIRY
LANTERNS

YELLOW
GLOBE LILY

YELLOW MARIPOSA

SIERRA
STAR TULIP

BLUE STAR TULIP

SEGO LILY

DESERT MARIPOSA

YELLOW
STAR TULIP

WHITE
MARIPOSA

Fairy Lanterns, Globe Lily, Snowdrops, Indian Bells, Satin Bells, *Calochortus albus*   The petals of this Lily turn together to form a very lovely globe, with the glands forming humps on the outside. Blossoms and light green buds droop on slender stems. The capsule is 1-2 inches (2.5-5 cm) long and almost as beautiful as the blossoms as it develops into a three-sided, dainty, pale green, nodding fruit.

Calochortus pulchellus is a yellow species very much like fairy lanterns. Both grow in California.

Yellow Mariposa, *Calochortus luteus,* blooms late in spring in fields and hills. It is an upright, bright yellow tulip. It is the most abundant Lily in California.

Sierra Star Tulip, *Calochortus nudus,* is white with a pinkish-purple spot and light blue anthers. It grows in coniferous forests of the Sierra Nevada up to 7,000 feet. It is small and its one broad leaf grows longer than the flower stem.

Blue Star Tulip, Beaver Tailed Grass, *Calochortus caeruleus,* is white or pale blue with lilac dots and lined with blue hairs. Found in northern Coast Ranges of California, south to San Diego.

Sego Lilies, *Calochortus nuttallii,* grow in the dry ranges bordering the deserts of southern California, in the Rocky Mountains, and east to the Dakotas, 4,000-10,000 feet. They are so abundant and lovely in Utah that they have been named the state flower. They are white, sometimes shaded with lilac or purple, with a dark purple spot and yellow anthers. The petals are often crinkled at the edges. Used as food by Indians and early settlers.

Yellow Star Tulip, *Calochortus monophyllus,* is deep yellow, tiny, and very hairy with a reddish-brown spot. It opens up very wide and is sometimes called yellow pussy ears because it is so fuzzy. Found in the pine belt of Sierra Nevada from Shasta to Yosemite.

Desert Mariposa, *Calochortus kennedyi,* is a brilliant orange-red flame-colored flower with brown spots and brownish-purple anthers. The sepals are pale green, bordered with pink on the outside, but orange-red inside. Grows by the thousands in Arizona, also in California's Mojave Desert, west to Ventura.

White Mariposa, *Calochortus venustus,* has a vivid maroon, orange, and crimson spot on each petal. Sepals are striped with pink and dark red, and pale purple anthers curve around the purple pistil. Found in northern Coast Ranges south to Los Angeles, and in Sierra Nevada. A number of other Mariposas are similar; commonly called butterfly tulips.

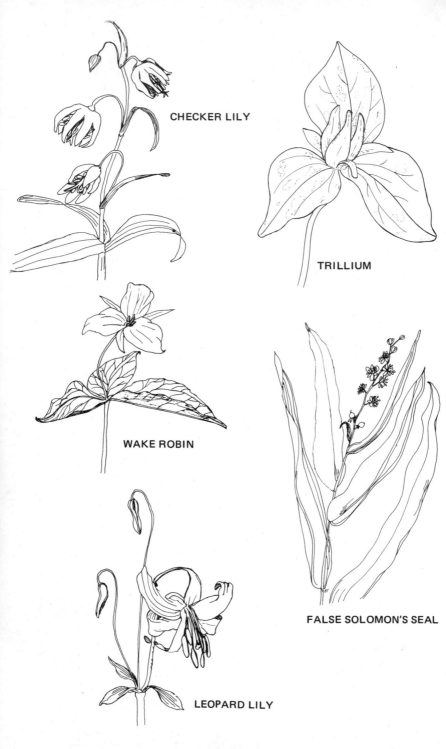

CHECKER LILY

TRILLIUM

WAKE ROBIN

FALSE SOLOMON'S SEAL

LEOPARD LILY

44

Checker Lily, Mission Bells, Leopard Lily, *Fritillaria lanceolata,* has hanging, bell-shaped flowers. Both petals and sepals are dark purple, dotted with greenish yellow, with a dark green line extending through the length of each. Found in southern California north into Canada, east to mountains of Utah and Idaho. *Fritillaria atropurpurea* is similar with smaller blossoms. It is mostly in Rocky Mountains, but can be found all over the West.

TRILLIUMS are different from other Lilies in that they have netted-veined leaves. Three large green leaves grow whorled around the stout unbranched stem just below the single three-petal flower. They bloom early on moist hillsides or in canyons of California's Coast Ranges to Canada, in the Sierra, and Rocky Mountains from Montana to Colorado, and are found abundantly in the East.

Trilliums are among the first spring flowers all over the country and in many places are protected by law. If the flower is picked the perennial rootstalk will die because the only leaves are those located just under the flower.

Wake Robin, *Trillium ovatum,* is a white trillium with petals 1-2 inches (2.5-5 cm) across. Blooms from February to April in shady canyons near the coast from Monterey, California, to British Columbia and east to Idaho. Blossoms turn pink with age.

Trillium chloropetalum (sessile var. *giganteum*) has several variations. The deep maroon variety grows in central California, the greenish variety is found farther north.

False Solomon's Seal, Star Flower, *Smilacina stellata,* is noticed for its fresh green lance-shaped leaves which clasp the stem; the white blossoms form starry clusters at the tip of an unbranched stem. Found in Sierra Nevada and Coast Ranges to Washington. The fruit is a green berry stripped with black. *Smilcina racemesa* is a taller, broader leafed species in the Rockies, with red-mottled berries.

Tiger Lily, Leopard Lily, *Lilium paradalinum,* has big bright orange blossoms with a lighter orange center and purple spots on petals and sepals which curve back from the very noticeable long stamens. Many dramatic flowers grow on plants 3-7 feet (.9-2.1 m) tall. Leaves grow in whorls of ten to twenty, forming tiers along the stem. Grows along streams and most areas in mountains all over the West to 4,000 feet. Very like the wood lily of the East and yellow lily meadow of the North.

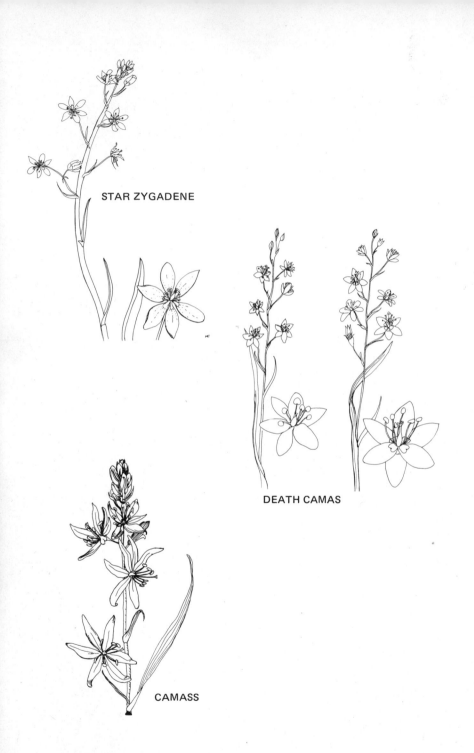

STAR ZYGADENE

DEATH CAMAS

CAMASS

Star Zigadene, *Zigadenus fremontii,* has many white or greenish-yellow
star-shaped flowers with conspicuous dark gland spots at base of petals;
the stamens are shorter than the petals. Flowers grow in racemes on stems
1-2 feet (30-60 cm) tall above the long narrow basal leaves from bulbs,
petals persisting after withering. The fruit is a three-part capsule.
Zigadenes are found all over the West; some species grow in wet meadows
in the Coast Ranges, and the Sierra and Rocky Mountains, others on
sagebrush hills bordering the deserts or on alkaline flats.

Death Camas is poisonous to cattle and sheep and man. *Zigadenus elegans* is
the high mountain death camas found in damp meadows at 6,000-12,000
feet. They have definite heart-shaped glands at the base of cream-colored
petals and sepals. *Zigadenus venenosus* is found in middle altitudes. Most
poisoning occurs early in the spring, because these plants tend to grow
before the regular range plants. Both of these species have stamens longer
than petals.

DEATH CAMAS and CAMASS, a lovely blue nonpoisonous lily,
described below, must not be confused. While in bloom, they
don't look at all alike, although before or after they might be
confused. The camass grows taller, more individually, with fewer
and broader leaves. Leaves of death camas are quite grass-like and
the individual leaves seem to grow right from the bulb. The outer
bulb coats of both are mostly dark or black, but this outer membranous coat extends up the stem for a distance of two or three times the
bulb diameter in the Zigadenes. The dark bulb covering on camass
terminates at the bulb top or just a bit above it. It should never be
eaten unless positive identification is made—easiest when in bloom.

Camass, *Camassia quamash*   Camass has beautiful bright blue flowers,
arranged along a 1-2 foot (30-60 cm) tall unbranched stem with basal
leaves as wide as 1 inch (2.5 cm). Found in wet meadows and streambanks, 4,500-6,500 feet, from Canada to California and Utah. It may be
scattered or grow in great masses. The three sepals and three petals are
colored alike, ½-¾ inch (1.3-1.8 cm) long, each with a stamen on its
base, the anthers swinging freely. Each petal and sepal withers and twists
separately. *Camassia leichtlinii* has deeper blue flowers that appear even
more star-like, but the withered petals twist together over the developing
capsule. Blooms in June and July. Camass affected early western history
more than any other plant. The bulb is very starchy and edible at all times,
but tastes best in the fall. They were eaten raw, baked, dried, or roasted by
Indians, early trappers, explorers and settlers. The Chief Joseph War was
started because the Clearwater Indians went south, out of their area, to
collect bulbs. The Indian name was *quamash.*

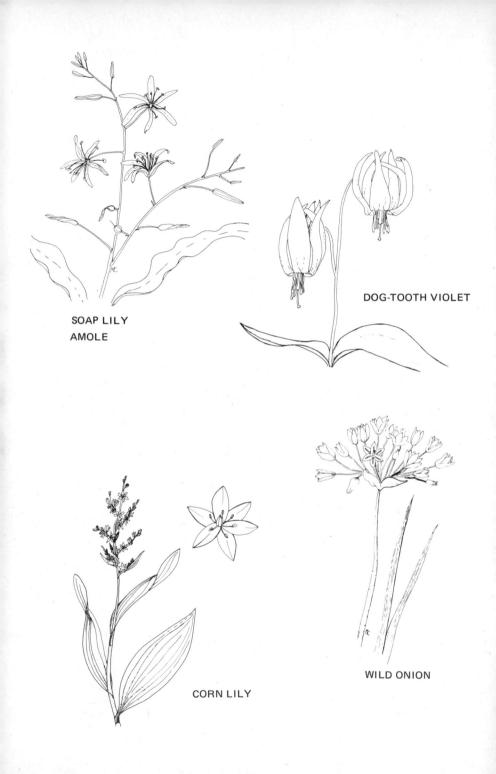

SOAP LILY
AMOLE

DOG-TOOTH VIOLET

CORN LILY

WILD ONION

48

Soap Lily, Amole, *Chlorogalum pomeridianum*   This conspicuous 2-8 foot (.6-2.4 m) summer-blooming plant with small, pretty white flowers is noticeable in late afternoon when the blue-gray buds open. The narrow petals and sepals are alike, lined with purple veins. They bloom, in successive evenings, from the lower branches to the tip, the flowers looking like tiny ballerinas. The petals wither by morning, twisting over the developing round capsule which produces many seeds. The leaves are basal and are long and narrow with rippling edges, often dried by flowering time. The bulb grows near the surface, and is heavily covered with fibers. The bulb will form a lather in water after the fibers are pulled off. Spanish-Americans and Indians used them for soap. They also ate them, cooking them in ground pits. It is found on dry open hills and plains of California and southern Oregon; also found in desert regions.

Fawn Lily, Glacier Lily, Dog-Tooth Violet, *Erythronium grandiflorum,* is one of the loveliest, best-known and earliest of the spring flowers, growing in moist woodlands, meadows, moist rocky slopes, and streambanks over much of the West; you can even find them in August in the mountains near melting snowbanks. The clear yellow petals and sepals are colored alike, the parts bending backwards showing the six stamens, the three-parted stigma and three-parted superior ovary. Two or three flowers are borne on slender stalks between the two shiny, often mottled, leaves from a deep bulb. *Erythronium californicum* is similar and common in California at 500-3,500 feet. Flowers are white, cream, or yellowish; leaves are brown-mottled.

Corn Lily, False Hellebore, Skunk Cabbage, *Veratrum californicum,* is a tall strikingly characteristic plant of high wet meadows or spring areas 4,500-8,500 feet. The big, heavily veined leaves appear pleated. The flowers are small and yellowish, but are arranged in a tall flowering stalk above the leafy stem, making the plant very noticeable. Stamens are short but curve outwards, making them conspicuous. Grows from a short, thick rootstock. Very unlike the eastern (or true western) skunk cabbage, but the name is used, nevertheless. The young shoots are poisonous to browsing sheep and to humans, particularly when eaten in quantity.

Wild Onion, *Allium unifolium,* grows all over the West. There are many different species but all are characterized by many small flowers, clustered into an umbel. When in bud, the umbel is covered with two thin papery bracts which remain after the flowers open. Blossoms resemble Brodieaeas, but are white, pink, or rose-color, and have a strong onion odor. Indians used the bulbs for food. *Allium unifolium* is a lavender-pink species.

BRODIAEAS are much like ALLIUM with flowers growing in umbels at the top of a naked stem. The flowers usually are blue, white, or golden. The calyx and corolla are united near the base. The

BLUE DICKS

(Brodiaea pulchella)

(Brodiaea douglasii)

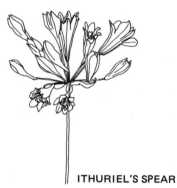

ITHURIEL'S SPEAR

HARVEST BRODIAEA

GOLDEN BRODIAEA

long, narrow leaves dry early. There are about twenty species. The bulbs were a source of food for Indians.

Blue Dicks, *Brodiaea pulchella (capitata),* grows in open fields or among oaks on hillsides and mountains to 4,000 feet, blooming early in California, Oregon, Arizona and New Mexico. The flower head has four to ten separate flowers, the flower cluster is surrounded at the base by small metallic-purple bracts. The sepals and petals are purplish-blue. The three stamens opposite the petals have "wings" on the filaments; the other three anthers are much smaller, *Brodiaea douglasii* is also called blue dick, but the flowers are not in a tight head, each peduncle from 1/16-1/8 inches (2-3 mm) long. They grow from San Francisco to Washington, east to the Rockies. Both have edible bulbs, raw, boiled, or roasted.

Ithuriel's Spear, Grass Nut, Wally Basket, *Brodiaea laxa,* is the largest and best known of the Brodiaeas. The flowers grow in a loose umble, not a tight cluster as in blue dick. There are many beautiful, showy flowers, each growing on a short, bent pedicel, facing upwards. There usually are eight to thirty flowers in each umbel, sometimes as many as forty-eight. The petals and sepals are blue-violet; the filaments are thread-like, not winged; the ovary is on a long stem. This plant grows from a corm. The Indians dug these corms and ate them for their nut-like flavor. This beautiful, common Brodiaea blooms from April to June all over California, especially in adobe soil areas.

Harvest Brodiaea, *Brodiaea coronaria,* is a beautiful clear blue or blue-violet with a dark line down the center of each petal and sepal; there are only three to ten flowers in each umbel. The flowers open wide, showing three tall stamens and three staminodia. The ovary is angled, showing its three parts even from the outside. Harvest brodiaea are common in the foothills along the Central Valley of California and from Oregon to southern California in the coastal hill and valley areas. The flowers can be found in late May and June at the time of the hay harvest when the fields are turning brown.

Golden Brodiaea, *Brodiaea lutea (ixioides),* has sixteen to forty star-like flowers, growing in umbels on a slender, tough stem 6-18 inches (15-45 cm) tall. It is common in the grassy foothill fields, but also grows on the high hills and mountains of both the Coast Ranges and the Sierra. Each of the yellow petals and sepals has a black-purple line on the outside. The stamens also are yellow, with three tall ones alternating with three shorter ones. All of the filaments have broad wings, which seem to form a crown, with the anthers sitting like jewels in the notches. The ovary is on a short stem. The plant has two narrow leaves growing from the base. Golden brodiaea flowers late in the spring, May to June, later in the higher elevations. Sometimes it is in full bloom in late August around the last melting snowbanks.

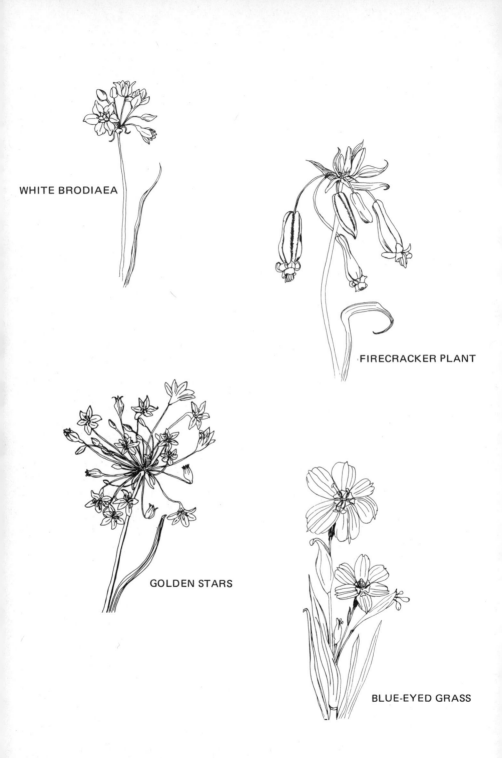

WHITE BRODIAEA

FIRECRACKER PLANT

GOLDEN STARS

BLUE-EYED GRASS

White Brodiaea, *Brodiaea hyacinthina,* grows thickly in meadows, especially around ponds or moist places in western valleys. Each petal and sepal of the ten-to-forty flower umbel has a distinct green midrib. The filaments are triangular and united at the base; the anthers are yellow or purple. The stem sometimes is only 6 inches (15 cm) high, but may be as tall as 20 inches (50 cm). The grass-like leaves are nearly as tall as the flowering stalk. They can be found in late spring from central California, north to Vancouver and eastward to the western Rocky Mountains.

Firecracker Plant, *Brodiaea ida-maia,* is not very abundant in the West, but it is such an unusual and attractive flower that most people want to know what it is when they do find it. It grows from 1,000-4,000 feet elevation, blooming in May to July, from San Francisco into southern Oregon. The flowers grow in umbels of six to twenty, each drooping downward. They have a bright red tube about an inch long (2.5 cm) which ends in a green six-lobe tip. These lobes turn up toward the red tube. There are three white stamens with pale yellow anthers, and three staminoidea. These are broadened so that they look like three white tiny petals. As the blossoms fade, and the capsules develop, they become erect.

Golden Stars, *Bloomeria crocea,* at first glance, could be mistaken for the golden brodieaea. However, the stamens of golden stars have long slender filaments of equal length, so the anthers are noticeable above the petals. In golden brodiaea, the filaments are broad and winged, alternately short and tall, the anthers appearing to sit as jewels on the "crown" made by the wide filaments. Golden stars has a nectar cup at the base of each filament and each sepal and petal has a narrow black midvein. Common in the southern Coast Ranges and mid Sierra Nevada of California.

IRIS FAMILY
Iridaceae

Iris flower parts are in threes, as are Lilies. The important difference is that a Lily has a superior ovary and in Iris, it is inferior. Also, Iris have only three stamens, while Lilies have six. Iris usually grow from creeping stout rootstocks. They have stout stems and sword-like leaves that straddle the stem or seem to wrap around it. Most wild Iris have a shape similar to that of the garden Iris, with the three sepals standing outwards or hanging down, the three petals standing up. Wild Iris grow all over America. The southern blue flag grows from Virginia into the Mississippi Valley. Other native Irises grow along the East Coast. Wild Iris is the state flower of Tennessee.

Blue-eyed Grass, Grass Widow, *Sisyrinchium bellum* does not have the typical Iris shape, but does have the Iris plan. Its purplish-blue sepals and petals are colored alike and all stand outwards. There is a bright yellow "eye" in the center. There are more than 100 species of blue-eyed grass, all natives of North or South America.

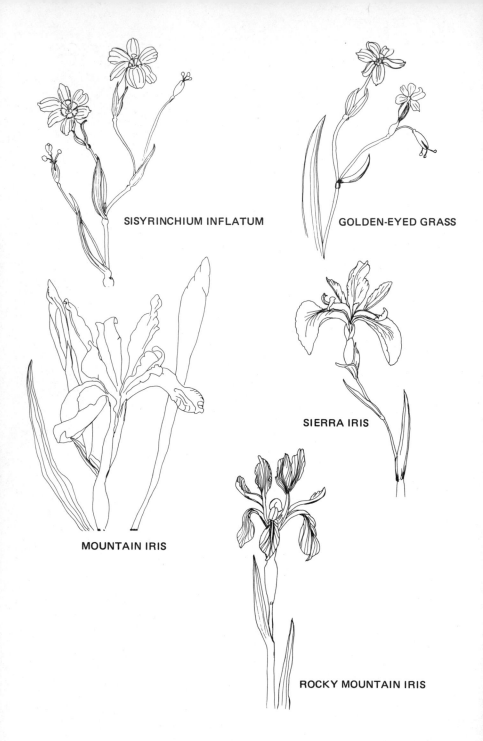

SISYRINCHIUM INFLATUM

GOLDEN-EYED GRASS

SIERRA IRIS

MOUNTAIN IRIS

ROCKY MOUNTAIN IRIS

Sisyrinchium inflatum is a bright purple or pink, large-flowered species which grows from British Columbia to Idaho, south to California and Nevada.

Golden-eyed Grass, *Sisyrinchium californicum,* has bright yellow flowers, and grows in California and Oregon. *Sisyrinchiam arizonicum* is another yellow species found in Arizona. *Sisyrinchiam elmeri* also is yellow, with purple lines, found in the Sierras. Very similar species grow in the East and Midwest, and are recognized easily as related to the Western species.

Mountain Iris, *Iris douglasiana,* with typical Iris shape, is common in the Coast Ranges of Oregon and California. They may be lavender or blue, cream or pinkish white, sometimes striped with yellow or veined with purple.

Sierra Iris, *Iris hartwegii,* is smaller, yellow with lavender veins, or pale lavender, or blue with deeper-colored veins, with the middle of the petal a lovely yellow. Found in dry forests, 2,500-6,000 Sierras to Lower California.

Rocky Mountain Iris, Western Blue Flag, *Iris missouriensis,* is a lovely pale blue or lavender, and the only one found in the Rocky Mountains. Grows in great masses in damp meadows from low valleys to 9,000 feet, in Rockies, east to the Dakotas, west to British Columbia, Sierras, north Coast Ranges, south to New Mexico. Ground Iris, *Iris macrosiphon,* is a beautiful Iris that is violet-purple, straw-yellow, or veined or spotted with white. It grows from 100-3,000 feet elevation in the Coast Ranges from central California into Oregon, January through spring. Indians used the narrow leaves to make ropes for catching small animals.

Chapter V

FLOWERS WITH FOUR PETALS

There are many western wildflowers with four petals. We have included the families that are most common in the West, plus some members of the Buttercup Family that have four petals, although most members of that family have five petals.

POPPY FAMILY
Papaveraceae

This is a large family, some growing as shrubs. Most Poppies have colored juice, showy flowers, and many stamens. There always are twice as many petals as sepals. In some species the sepals are united. In the genus *Eschscholtzia,* the calyx is shaped like a tall cap and falls off as the bud opens. All have one pistil, made of two or more parts, more or less united. The ovary is superior and is one-celled. The fruit is a long, slender capsule with many tiny seeds.

Members of the Poppy Family are found all over the world. The wild poppies of Europe and Asia are a bright red. Two lovely huge white poppies bloom in the Southwest, the matilija poppy and prickly poppy, but they have six petals so are described in Chapter X, as is cream cups, another member with six petals. Garden poppies include the bright Oriental poppies, Iceland poppies, and Shirley poppies; the California poppy is now planted in gardens around the world. The eastern blood root is a member of this family. Opium is produced from another species.

CALIFORNIA POPPY

BUSH POPPY

California Poppy, *Eschscholtzia californica,* is California's state flower. When the early settlers came this beautiful flower covered huge areas of the state. They were so colorful and widespread that they made landmarks for the ships at sea. Even today, they are widespread and are among the most loved of western wildflowers. The four petals are fan-shaped, large, brilliant orange to yellow, or, rarely, white. They open in bright sunlight only, closing to "sleep" in the evening or cloudy weather. The receptacle spreads into a red-edged ridge around the outside of the petals and makes an erect inner rim tightly holding the lower part of the ovary. The leaves are finely divided, gray-green, often reddish on new plants. Blooms with large spring flowers and again in summer with smaller, lighter colored flowers.

Bush Poppy, *Dendromecon rigida*   These poppies sometimes are called tree poppies because the bushes may be as high as 8 feet (2.4 m). The branches are woody, whitish, the main stem having shreddy bark. The blue-green leaves are rather long and narrow, quite pointed, stiff and leathery, resembling willow leaves. The leaf stalks twist so the leaves point upward. The blossoms resemble those of the California poppy. The four petals are golden yellow, the flowers 1-3 inches (2.5-7.5 cm) across and slightly fragrant. The many stamens have orange anthers; the pistil has two oblong pale yellow stigmas. There are two sepals. Bush poppies grow on dry, sunny ridges of California, at about 1,000-3,000 feet elevation, most of the length of the state, but rarely are found in the rest of the West.

MUSTARD FAMILY
Cruciferae

The Mustard Family has many genera and species and is widespread all over the world. It is easy to recognize these flowers as a family, but the different genera within the family cannot be recognized without the seed pods. The leaves and stems always have the characteristic mustard-like odor and juice. The flowers always have petals arranged in the shape of a cross, with the base of the petal (claw) quite narrow, the upper part (blade) wider and spreading out to make the four arms of the cross, giving the family name of *Cruciferae,* meaning cross or crucifix. There is great variation in the type of leaf, size of plants and color of flowers, but the above petal characteristics are true of all members of the family. The sepals sometimes are swollen or sac-like, making the petals look as though they were in a vase. There are six stamens, usually four long and two short. The ovary is superior, with one style, and one- or two-lobed stigma. The fruit usually is a two-celled capsule, which is long and narrow, or may be short and rounded. The seeds are tiny and numerous. Members of this family are: common yellow mustard,

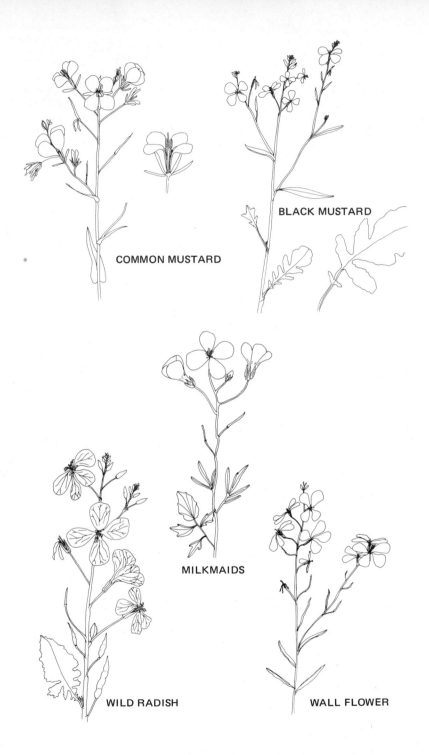

COMMON MUSTARD

BLACK MUSTARD

MILKMAIDS

WILD RADISH

WALL FLOWER

wild radish, milkmaids, fringe pod, peppergrass, shepherd's purse, jewel flower, wallflower, shield leaf. Many are grown for food as radish, turnip, cabbage, cauliflower, watercress. Mustard, as a condiment, is ground up mustard seeds. Some are common garden plants as candy tuft, stock, and alyssum.

Common Yellow Mustard, *Brassica campestris,* makes fields and orchards bright each spring all through California. The flowers are clear yellow, scattered thickly along the branching stems, which may be 1-6 feet (30-180 cm) high. At the base of each yellow petal is a round green gland. As the flowers fade, seed pods begin forming. The lower part of the branches become covered with slender pods. The leaves all are clasping on the stems; many people gather very young ones to use as a green vegetable. It may bloom as early as January, continuing to April and later in irrigated fields.

Black Mustard, *Brassica nigra,* grows up to 12 feet (3.6 m) tall, and is common throughout the Pacific Northwest, in fact, all over North America except in the extreme North. The lower leaves are very divided resembling the leaves of wild radish and not at all like field mustard. The flowers are much smaller, also. Its seeds produce a valuable antiseptic oil. Indians roasted mustard seeds, then ground them into meal which was made into cakes or added to soup or to flavor cornmeal.

Wild Radish, *Raphanus sativus,* has petals that are white, pinkish, purplish, or pale yellow, with many purplish veins. The plant branches more than the yellow mustard, and grows 2-5 feet (60-150 cm) high. The thick white root smells and tastes like the radishes we eat, but with a stronger flavor. The plant often covers fields and orchards, sometimes growing with the yellow mustards, blooming in March and April.

Milkmaids, Toothwort, *Dentaria californica,* is the loveliest of all the Mustards. They have dainty little flowers of white or pale rose-color, on plants 6-24 inches (15-60 cm) tall. They usually grow with just one stem from the tuberous rootstock. The large thin leaves are very pretty, varying from rounded basal leaves to stem leaves which are indented into three to five leaflets, sometimes purple beneath. Grows on shady banks or in wooded spots on the hills, 200-8,700 feet. Other species grow in moist places in the valleys, from central California into Oregon. Related species are found in the woods of the eastern and central states.

Wallflower, *Erysimum asperum,* is a very handsome plant with its big, bright orange, crowded raceme of four-petal orange-yellow flowers. The stem is thick and stiff, 1-3 feet (30-90 cm) tall, with long, narrow leaves. Other varieties of wallflower are in various shades of yellow. Some plants are no more than 6 inches (15 cm) tall. They grow all over the West, and as far east as Ohio; many of them are found in Europe and Asia. They earned the name of wallflower by growing in cracks of old stone walls, especially in Europe.

JEWEL FLOWER

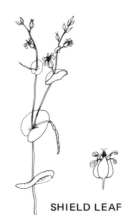

SHIELD LEAF

FRINGEPOD

WATERCRESS

Jewel Flower, *Streptanthus glandulosus,* has rows of little blossoms all down the stems like strings of jewels. Three of the sepals tend to stick together at the tip, with the lower one spreading out. They are deep amethyst color, the petals lighter, even white, with purple veins. Leaves are arrowhead shape, with stiff hairs. Blooms in dry open hills of California April through June.

Shield Leaf, *Streptanthus tortuosus,* has rounded, curved leaves, like a heart-shaped shield. They are sessile and clasping on the branching, twisted stems, which may be 3-36 inches (7.5-90 cm) high. As the plant natures, the upper leaves turn bright yellow, like brassy shields. The flowers are unique. The four sepals are purplish and saccate or swollen at the base and smaller at the top, with sepal tips curving outward. Petals are purplish or yellowish or white, with purple veins. As they fade, long slender curved pods develop, making the plant look peculiar. Found in the Sierra Nevada from central California to Mt. Shasta, 2,000-10,500 feet.

Fringepod, *Thysanocarpus curvipes*   The tiny white flowers are usually not noticed on this plant, but the seed pod is quite attractive. The superior ovary is one-celled and becomes a winged round pod crowded with broad rays. As the pod matures, the membranous areas between the rays dry or disintegrate, so the pod appears fringed. These seed pods may be colored in some varieties. The plant grows 12-18 inches (30-45 cm) high, with numerous narrow, mainly basal, leaves. Common in open hill areas from California north to British Columbia.

Watercress, Cress, Pepperleaf, *Nasturtium officinale (Rorippa nasturtium-aquaticum),* is familiar to many people who either know its green leafiness in springs and streams or buy it at their markets. They may never have seen or noticed its tiny white, but typical, flowers. The plant grows along, and floating in, cold streams, often forming dense mats. Masses of white roots, looking like threads, grow downward from the stem where the lower leaves branch off. The leaves are pinnately compound with three to nine leaflets. They have a bitey-tangy flavor, and have been known and eaten by people since ancient times.

Watercress was brought to this country by Europeans, escaped from cultivation, and is now found naturalized in the mountains over most of the country in clear cold streams or springs. It blooms from May to August. Late in the season it may become very strongly flavored. Its old name, translated, means "nose twister that grows along stream edges."

CAPER FAMILY
Capparidaceae

The Caper Family is very similar to the Mustard Family in growth, flower structure, and heavily-scented leaves, though in this family, the scent may be unpleasant and strong rather than pungent or

CLEOME

mustard-like. The leaves are usually palmately compound, with three leaflets. The four sepals are much smaller than the four petals (and are not clawed as in most of the Mustard Family). The six stamens are of about the same length (definitely *not* four long and two short as in Mustards), and are much longer than the petals. The ovary is one- or two-celled, on a stalk that lengthens as the ovary matures.

Cleome, Rocky Mountain Bee Plant, Stink Weed, Spider Plant, Bean Plant, *Cleome serrulata* (pink-lavender or white), *Cleome lutea* (yellow), is a strong-smelling flower found over most of the West, Arizona to Washington and east to the Rocky Mountains, growing along roadsides, waste area, and fields to 6,000 feet. The flowers are fairly small, ¼-½ inch (6-13 mm), but grow in a raceme with buds at the top, then many open flowers, and the developing seed pods below. The ovary is on a short stalk which lengthens as the ovary matures, so the pods hang. This flower is much like a Mustard in structure, but the stamens are all very long, extending beyond the petals and giving the flower a feathery-soft appearance. The much-branched plant grows 2-5 feet (60-150 cm) tall, and usually many bees are around it. It blooms from May to August, depending on altitude. It is often seen along the transcontinental roads of the West, common in the Southwest, but found also in the central and northern United States. The pink species has leaves that are three-parted; the yellow species has leaves divided into five to seven leaflets.

EVENING PRIMROSE FAMILY
Onagraceae

Only a few of the plants of the Evening Primrose Family bloom at night or look like primroses, so it is not a very good name. It is, however, an extremely interesting family. The ovary is inferior, and often so far below the flower that it is mistaken for part of the stem. The four sepals are united into a calyx tube which has a long "neck" above the ovary, with the tips bending outwards as the buds open. The four petals are often quite showy or bright. Flowers in this family are yellow or creamy or rose to deep pink, often two-color (as in Fuchsias). There are eight stamens and four stigmas; this is the "plan of four" as the Mustard and Caper Families have. The important clue is that the ovary is inferior, making this family definitely distinguishable. The pollen usually is cobwebby and sticky. Plants often are tall, with many flowers in a raceme, or may be low-growing with the leaves all basal, forming a rosette. It is a widely distributed family, with many species in the West. It is an

CLARKIA (C. UNGUICULATA)

CLARKIA (C. PULCHELLA)

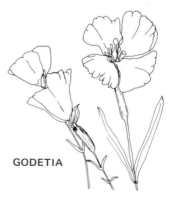

GODETIA

easy family to recognize, although many members look very much like Mustards until you examine them for these clues:

1. Is the ovary inferior (as Evening Primrose) or superior (as Mustard)?

2. Are there eight stamens (as Evening Primrose) or six stamens (four long, two short as in Mustards)?

Clarkia, *Clarkia unguiculata,* is such a lovely annual wildflower that it often is planted in gardens. The four rose-pink petals have long claws with the blades often divided or lobed. The petals spread far apart, often turning and standing as two pairs. The flowers grow in racemes, the buds drooping or nodding until they open. The seeds develop in a long four-angled capsule. The brittle-stemmed plants grow 12-25 inches (30-60 cm) high. Grows in Coast Range hills, Mendocino County to southern California, and in the Sierra Nevada hills, flowering in late spring.

Clarkia pulchella is abundant in the Rocky Mountain valley and foothill areas up to 6,000 feet, turning whole hillsides pink during a good season, also from California north to British Columbia. The petals are three-lobed, the flowers 1-1½ inches (2.5-4 cm) across, growing in clusters on plants 6-20 inches (15-50 cm) high. The genus was named for Captain Clark of the Lewis and Clark party, because it was first collected in 1806 along the Clearwater River in Idaho when he explored from the Rocky Mountains to the Pacific.

Godetia, Summer's Darling, Farewell-to-Spring, Herald-to-Summer, *Clarkia amoena*   Godetias are similar to the common Clarkias, but the petals are broad at the base, rounded at the tip, and have no claws. There are many different species; their common names tell us they bloom at the end of the spring flower season. The showy flowers are purple, rose or lavender-pink, quite large and often splashed with a dark red or purple spot on each petal. They form bright spots of color in the drying grass, looking something like mallow from a distance; the blossoms close at night. The four sepal tips turn back above the inferior ovary, and often are the same color as the petals. The leathery capsule is four-sided or ribbed, about an inch (2.5 cm) long. It splits open when dry, releasing many seeds. The plants have slender stems, few branches and grow 9-39 inches (23-100 cm) tall. The flowers grow closely along the stem, the buds erect. The leaves are long and narrow, growing alternately on the stem. Godetias are common in the foothills of the Sierra and Coast Ranges. They grow naturally only in California, but are found in many gardens; seed companies have developed large double-flowered forms. Blooms in June and July.

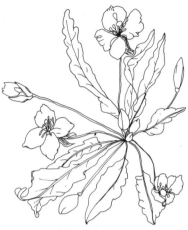

SUNCUP

WHITE EVENING PRIMROSE

Sun Cups, Golden Eggs, *Oenothera ovata,* have brilliant glistening yellow flowers close to the flat rosette of large leaves and bloom from February to April in fields and valleys from mid-California to southern Oregon. The ovary is so low in this flower that it actually is partly underground. The long part of the calyx, surrounding the style below the flower, appears to be the stem. The four pointed tips of the calyx are yellow-green, and turn back just under the golden petals. The four rounded petals are ½ inch (1.3 cm) long, the stigma knoblike, and the eight stamens have cobwebby pollen. The large flat rosette of leaves can be identified in the fields as soon as the rains begin. It grows much like the basal leaves of filaree, but these leaves are quite large, 3-6 inches (7.5-15 cm) long, entire, with a wavy margin, not finely divided as in filaree. Usually only the central rib is reddish. The ½ inch (1.3 cm) long capsule is mostly underground. This makes seed distribution rather a problem, but the pod opens late, after the leaves are turning brown and shriveled, so they are out of the way. Also, it grows mostly in adobe soils which develop cracks as they dry.

EVENING PRIMROSE.   There are many evening primroses, all somewhat similar, growing all over the world. Some of them are white, many are yellow, petals often turning pinkish as they wither. All open in late afternoon or evening, lasting through part or all of the next day.

White evening Primrose, *Oenothera caespitosa*   This low-growing plant has large, lovely white flowers that are 2-4 inches (5-10 cm) across, turning pinkish as they grow older. Each flower appears to have a slender stem, but this really is the extremely long calyx tube, 2-4 inches (5-10 cm) long, which leads to the inferior ovary down in the basal rosette of leaves. The flower is cup-like with each of the large petals heart-shaped. The yellow stamens are attached to the thickened base of the petals. The swinging anthers are attached to the filament by their middle and produce quantities of cobwebby pollen which hang in threads. The style and four-branched stigma also are yellow, the style longer than the stamens. Grows on slopes and in washes, 2,000-7,000 foot elevations, eastern Oregon, south to western Nevada and California.

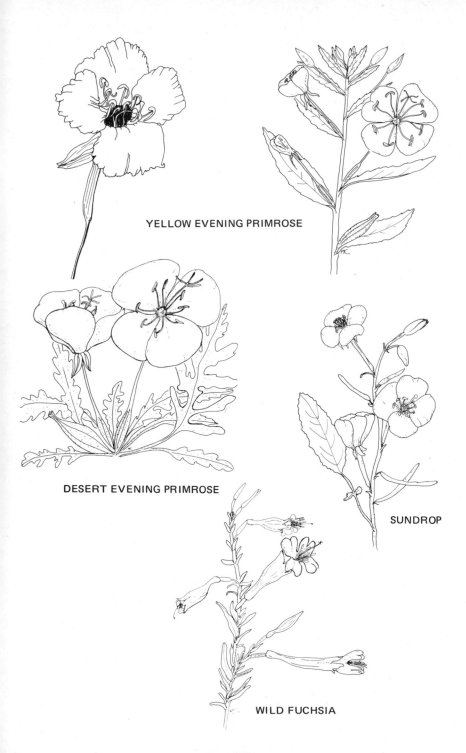

YELLOW EVENING PRIMROSE

DESERT EVENING PRIMROSE

SUNDROP

WILD FUCHSIA

Yellow Evening Primrose, *Oenothera hookeri, Oenothera rydbergii*   These two bright yellow fragrant Evening Primroses are much alike, with the petals of *Oenothera hookeri* 1-2 inches (2.5-5 cm) wide and long while those of *Oenothera rydbergii* are only ½-1 inch (1.3-2.5 cm) wide. *Oenothera hookeri,* with its larger petals, is a very showy flower; it is mainly a California species. The other species is found over the large area from Minnesota and Kansas west to the Pacific along moist lowlands, streams and in grassy areas up to 5,000 feet. Both have swinging anthers, cobwebby pollen, and sessile capsules. The lower part of the stem will have fairly mature capsules while buds are still developing at the top. The capsules appear granular on their shiny green surface and remain as dry cases on the old stalks through the winter. The erect plants grow from 2-4 feet (60-150 cm) high, with thick stalks. The leaves are 4-9 inches (10-22.5 cm) long. Stalk, leaves, and buds are covered with soft, downy white hairs. The buds grow erect on their stems, the calyx tips showing red. The flowers are in the axils of the leaves.

Desert Evening Primrose,*Oenothera primiveris,*has very similar flowers but is low-growing, with the flowers among the basal rosette of hairy leaves, not on a tall stalk. The petals are 1-1-1/8 inches (2.5-2.8 cm) long and wide. It is a desert species, found in western Texas, across to California.

Sundrop, *Oenothera brevipes*   This beautiful yellow Evening Primrose is found all over the deserts of the West. It varies in height from 4 inches (10 cm) to several feet, depending on moisture and depth of soil. The blossoms are delicate and lovely. The petals are golden yellow, each about ½ inch (1.3 cm) wide; the petal tips seem cut off, so the blossom looks squarish. The anthers swing; the style is threadlike with a round greenish stigma. This round stigma is one of the distinguishing characteristics of this species, for others have a four-parted stigma.

The calyx is on a short pedicel. The blossoms grow in a dense terminal spike which droops at the tip in the bud stage. The flowers wilt soon after sunrise, turning pink or red. It develops long capsules which are squarish. The stems are thick and covered with long soft hairs. The leaves may be long and often have small lobes on the petioles. In the warmer deserts, sundrops begin to bloom in February, but they are found more commonly from March to May in the desert washes of the West, from 100-7,000 feet elevation.

Wild Fuchsia, Hummingbird Trumpet, California Balsamea, *Zauschneria californica*   This brilliant scarlet flower is found in gray-leaved clumps on rocky or dry hillsides. The flower is like a scarlet trumpet with an abrupt bulge at the top of the inferior ovary, gradually bulging again to the base of the colored sepal tips, then flaring. The petals are attached to the inner surface of the calyx tube at this level. Each of the petals is notched at the tip so at first glance the flower appears to be eight-petaled. The long stamens and style also are bright red and extend beyond the petals, the four-part stigma forming a small cross. The beautiful flower is 1-1½

FIREWEED

inches (2.5-3.8 cm) long above the dark red ovary. As the flower withers, it falls off as a unit, the capsule then lengthening and becoming more four-sided. The seeds are oblong, each tipped with a tuft of hairs. The clump is often spreading, with flowers on each branch tip. The leaves are sessile, small and narrow, hairy or glandular. This is a perennial plant, becoming woody at the base and the bark tending to peel. It grows easily from seed and makes a lovely garden flower. Blooms all summer and well into the fall months. Found on dry hillsides, and rock areas from 50-5,000 feet from southern California northward. A very similar species. *Zauschneria garrettii,* is found on dry canyon slopes and rock ledges all through the Rocky Mountains.

Fireweed, Willowherb, *Epilobium angustifolium,* is one of the most colorful and common wildflowers. This lovely rose-colored flower is found from low valleys to tree line, wherever the soil is moist enough, across North America, Europe and Asia. It often covers huge areas, and is one of the first flowers to come in after a burn; from this it received its name. The other common name comes from its willow-like leaves and abundant cottony seeds. These airborne seeds bring the plant quickly into barren or burned spots. They are often numerous enough to collect as tinder for starting fires.

The unbranched flower stalk is 2-6 feet (60-180 cm) tall, with lance-shaped leaves alternately arranged from the base to just below the showy raceme. The leaf veins are very characteristic, forming a scalloped design just inside the margin. The flowers are very showy, with even the drooping buds colored rose-purple. The sepal tips are narrow and purplish, and alternate with the petals, which are ½ inch (1.3 cm) long and stand out with the tips curved up. The eight purple stamens droop, but until the pollen is dispersed the style is so bent downwards it almost touches the sepal between the two lower petals. As the pollen drops, the style lifts up and the white four-parted stigma opens. The flower stands at the top of the inferior ovary, which develops into a purplish capsule by fall; the leaves also turn autumn colors. Young tender shoots can be used in salads or cooked for greens; dry leaves can be used for tea.

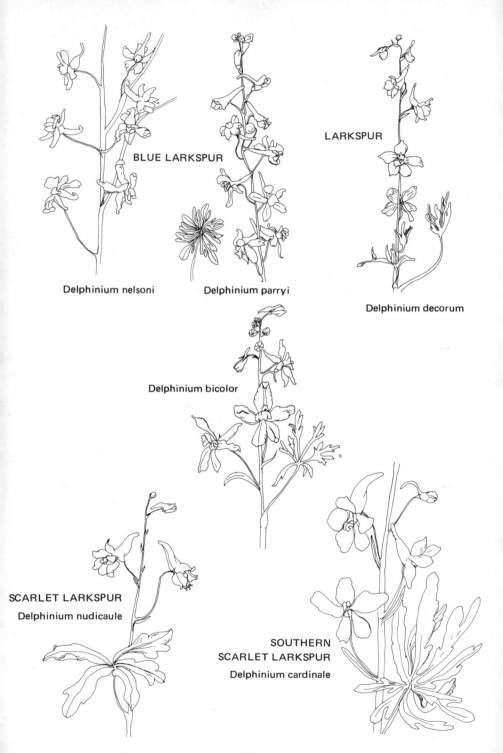

BLUE LARKSPUR

LARKSPUR

Delphinium nelsoni

Delphinium parryi

Delphinium decorum

Delphinium bicolor

SCARLET LARKSPUR

Delphinium nudicaule

SOUTHERN
SCARLET LARKSPUR

Delphinium cardinale

74

BUTTERCUP FAMILY
Ranunculaceae

Larkspur, *Delphinium*   Most of the Buttercup Family are described in chapters VI and VII, because the number of their petals
make them fit there. Larkspur are unusual members, but follow the
general family pattern. There are many species of larkspur which
grow in the West. All resemble one another in shape, which is
similar to those found all over the world, including the garden
varieties. A larkspur is easy to recognize because of the peculiar
shape of the blossom. As the name indicates, it has a long spur at the
back, which really is one of the five sepals. The sepals are colored
like the petals. Their color may be purple, blue, violet, white, pink,
red, scarlet, or various shades of these colors, or even multicolored.
There are four petals in unequal pairs, with the upper ones having
spurs which are hidden in the long sepal spur. The blossoms grow on
a long spike at the tip of each branch. In some species, individual
blossoms may be as large as an inch (2.5 cm) or more across. Others
are smaller, but all are very attractive. The many eastern species are
closely related. Many large-petal varieties have been developed for
gardens.

Delphinium nelsoni has deep blue-purple flowers, and is found from South
   Dakota to Idaho and south through Colorado and Utah from sagebrush
   areas to woods to mountains up to 10,000 feet elevation.

Delphinium parryi is a deep bright blue flower with purplish woolly spurs,
   purplish sepals, and the two upper petals white. It grows in southern
   California from the coast eastward.

Delphinium decorum, with purple-violet flowers, is the species most commonly found in the foothills of the Coast Ranges and the Sierra Nevada
   throughout California.

Delphinium bicolor grows in the Northwest east into Utah. Its spur is purple,
   the other sepals have some pink, and the two upper petals are white striped
   with purple.

Scarlet Larkspur, *Delphinium nudicaule,* is brilliant red, tipped with yellow
   and grows from northern California to Washington. Its structure shows its
   relationship to columbine. It grows in shady and moist places.

Delphinium cardinale can be found in coastal southern California and into
   Mexico. Often mistaken for scarlet larkspur, it grows in much drier areas.
   Several desert species can be found in California, Arizona, and east into
   Texas. Low growing, they bloom in February and March. *Delphinium
   amabile* is the species which can grow with the least water.

GREEN GENTIAN

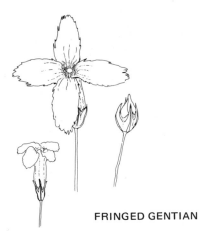

FRINGED GENTIAN

GENTIAN FAMILY
Gentianaceae

The Gentians are a family of lovely wildflowers. They appear in two places in this book (see page 125) because some species have four united petals and others have five united petals. Whichever number they have, the other flower parts follow that plan. The green gentian and the fringed gentian each have four united petals so are in this chapter.

Green Gentian, Deer's Tongue, Frasera, *Swertia radiata (Frasera speciosa)*, is a striking 2-6 foot (60-180 cm) tall, leafy, unbranched plant with whorls of large lance-shaped leaves all along the stem. The pale green glossy stem is very thick, sometimes 2 inches (5 cm) at the base. The flowers are on pedicels from axils of the upper leaf whorls. Individually they are fairly small, ¾-1½ inches (1.9-3.8 cm) across, but there are so many, crowded on the upper part of the stem, that they are very noticeable. The unusual greenish flowers have much symmetry and are marked with lines and dots of purple. Each petal lobe has two glands covered with fringed flaps; these form a four-sided pattern resembling the cultivated passion flower. The narrow sepals stand out straight, alternating with the broad petals which then alternate with the stamens. The first year a large characteristic clump of leaves grows; the second spring the flowering stalk is produced. It is found in the western mountains as far east as New Mexico and the Dakotas. Blooms begin in June; because of the number of flowers and the varying altitudes, many are still in bloom in August. They stand high above the grasses of the slopes, in open places of coniferous woods from 7,000-9,000 feet elevation.

Fringed Gentian, *Gentianaelegans (thermalis)*, is the annual gentian of the mountain meadws and streams from high foothills to 13,000 feet, especially in areas of warm springs. It is particularly abundant in Yellowstone National Park (where it it is the official flower), but is not found in Glacier National Park. Whole meadows are blue with it at the height of the season. The blue, lavender or purple flowers are 1-2 inches (2.5-5 cm) across, with four-fringed corolla lobes, twisted in the bud and still suggesting its twist when open. The calyx is angled, with lobes sharply pointed at the tip of the angles. There may be several stems from the base, but only one flower per stem; leaves are opposite. The fringed gentian blooms from June to August in the Rocky Mountains from Canada, south to Arizona and east to Idaho.

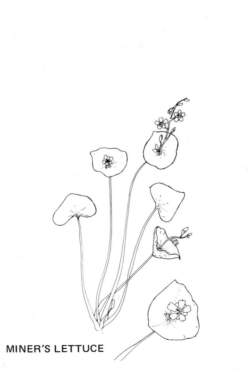

MINER'S LETTUCE

Chapter VI

FIVE SEPARATE PETALS
ALL ALIKE

Most of the flowers of the world have five petals, including a number of trees and shrubs, but there are many variations. This chapter contains just the flowers with five separate petals. Chapter VIII has the flowers with five petals which are at least partly united, and Chapter VII and IX contain flowers that have five petals not all the same shape.

PURSLANE FAMILY
Portulacaceae

Purslane is a family of low plants with rather thick juicy leaves. The regular, perfect flowers open only in bright sunshine, and wither quickly. Usually there are two sepals and five petals, but always there are fewer sepals than petals. The fruit is a capsule with two or three sections, or the top comes off like a lid. Garden portulaca and miner's lettuce are members of this family. Indians and early miners in the West commonly used miner's lettuce as a fresh green food. The wild members of this family most often seen are the lovely little red maids of California hillsides, the spring beauty of the mountains, and bitterroot (see page 00), the state flower of Montana.

Miner's Lettuce, Indian Lettuce, Squaw Cabbage, *Montia perfoliata,* has tiny, insignificant flowers held like a minute bouquet by the lovely succulent leaves, which are bright green and grow around the stem of the plant into a bowl-shape. These dainty, delicate plants are found all over the West, except in Arizona, growing in the thick leaf mold under trees and along streams. Excellent as salad greens.

RED MAIDS

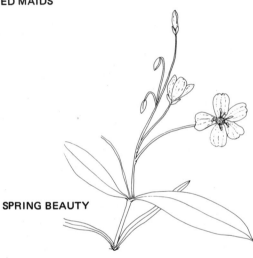

SPRING BEAUTY

Red Maids, *Calandrinia caulescens* var. *menziesii*, are an unusual and lovely shade of rose-red-purple, often carpeting whole hillsides and orchards. They make a brilliant patch in the sunshine, but would not be noticed on a cloudy day because they open only in full sunshine and remain open only a few hours before wilting. The plant is quite low, but spreads over the ground 6-24 inches (15-60 cm), with several flowers on each leafy branch. There are two sepals, five petals, and often five stamens, but different flowers on the same stem may have five to fourteen stamens. Blooms from late February through April from northern California into South America. Leaves excellent in green salads and as a pot herb.

Spring Beauty, Groundnut, *Claytonia lanceolata*, is usually the earliest spring wildflower of the mountains. It has pale pink or white petals, veined in deeper color, often with a spot of yellow at the base, and notched at the tip. Each reddish stem produces a pair of opposite succulent leaves near the top, with the flower stems coming from their base. The three-parted styles, the pistil and the five stamens are very noticeable and all are pink. It grows all over the West from 4,000-11,000 feet from northern California to British Columbia and east through the Rocky Mountains to New Mexico. It is an abundant wildflower of the East, also.

BUTTERCUP or CROWFOOT FAMILY
Ranunculaceae

The members of this family are hard to fit into a pattern. Most have five sepals, but the number of petals varies from zero to sixteen. The most dependable characteristic of the family is a cluster of separate pistils on a mound, surrounded by many stamens. Various members of the family do not seem to resemble one another, until they are examined for the family pattern, but there are exceptions to practically every family characteristic. They are herbs, except Clematis which is a vine; leaves are palmately divided, alternate or basal, except in Clematis where they are opposite; flowers are perfect, parts separate, free and distinct and usually regular, except Delphinium; blossoms grow one to a branch, except some are in racemes or panicles; usually there are five sepals, but always there are more than two and they may be petal-like as in Clematis; the number of stamens varies, even on the same plant; but the pistils are always separate, with the one-celled ovary superior; fruit is a pod, an achene, or (rarely) a berry. All these variations within the same family indicate a very simple, undeveloped kind of plant. Buttercups, one of the best known wildflowers, are among the earliest flowers found each spring. California buttercup has many petals, so is found in chapter X.

ALPINE BUTTERCUP

SAGEBRUSH BUTTERCUP

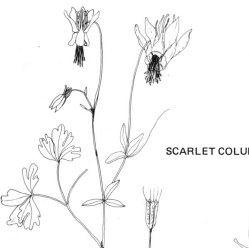

SCARLET COLUMBINE

ROCKY MOUNTAIN COLUMBINE

Sagebrush Buttercup, *Ranunculus glaberrimus,* blooms very early in sandy or gravelly valley areas, later in the season in the moist mountains. This species has much range of elevation and is found all over the West from British Columbia to the Rocky Mountains of Montana, south to California and Colorado. There are one to several yellow five-petal flowers on a stem, with many stamens and many pistils, and entire or three-lobed leaves.

Alpine Buttercup, *Ranunculus adoneus,* is the brilliant yellow buttercup found in the high mountains of the West. It is perennial and often the almost naked flowering stems poke up through the slush at the edge of melting snowbanks. Last year's dead leaves may still show at the base, this year's bright green leaves expanding at a later time. The five cup-shaped waxy petals are ¾-1 inch (1.9-2.5 cm) across. They are found at 9,500-11,500 feet in July and August.

COLUMBINES are strikingly beautiful members of the Buttercup Family. The flowers are very characteristic. The five colored sepals are petal-like and usually stand outwards. The five bright petals have long hollow spurs extending behind the calyx. The spurs have nectar, which attracts hummingbirds and bees. Since the spurs are so long, bees cannot reach the nectar; bumblebees cut holes in the spurs, making it possible for all bees to reach the nectar. are compound and each leaflet has two or three lobes or divisions. They are perennials common all over the United States and widely planted in gardens.

The clues which identify columbines as a member of the Buttercup Family are the many stamens (some of them may not have anthers), and the five separate simple pistils which develop into a head of five separate many-seeded pods.

Scarlet Columbine, *Aquilegia formosa,* is the scarlet columbine found so commonly in the mountains of California, Oregon and Washington, north to Alaska and east to Utah. The flowers hang down so the yellow spurs stand with closed ends up, the sepals spreading out flat, and the stamens dangling down. The branched plant grows from 1-3 feet (30-90 cm) high with light green leaves. Found commonly in moist woods from valleys to mountains. *Aquilegia truncata* is a similar columbine of shady valleys and hills of California.

Rocky Mountain Columbine, Blue Columbine, *Aquilegia coerulea,* is the state flower of Colorado. It is a large showy flower 1-3 inches (2.5-7.5 cm) across, with the big sepals white to light and deep blue, and the large spurred petals white to cream. The higher the altitude, the deeper the color; however, in Utah the flowers are almost pure white, only a few showing some color. They grow best on moist rocky slopes, high meadows, and along streams with aspen and spruce. Plants are 8-30 inches (20-75 cm) high, with long-stemmed leaves, mostly basal. They are among the loveliest and biggest of wildflowers, found in the high mountains of Colorado, Montana, Idaho, Utah, south to New Mexico.

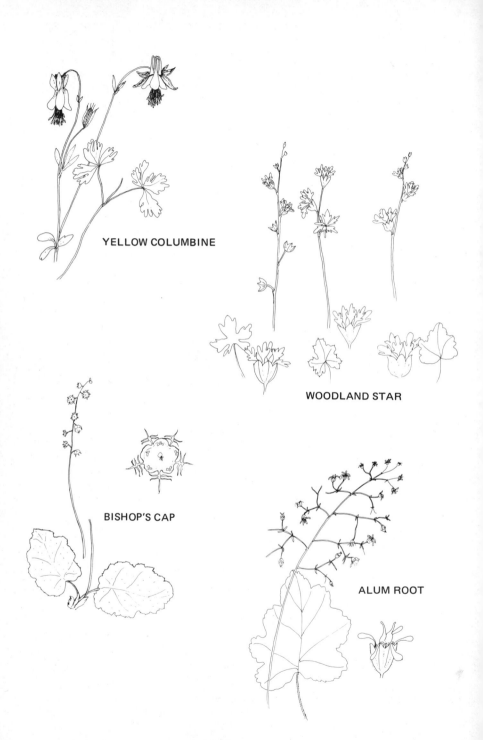

YELLOW COLUMBINE

WOODLAND STAR

BISHOP'S CAP

ALUM ROOT

Yellow Columbine, *Aquilegia flavescens,* is a common small-flowered columbine of open woods in the Rocky Mountain area west to British Columbia and south to Oregon, always found near streams. The yellowish sepals are longer than the cream-colored spurs and tend to turn back over the spurs. Many flowers grow on the branch stems, 3-4 feet (90-120 cm) tall.

SAXIFRAGE FAMILY
Saxifragaceae

The flowers are generally small and inconspicuous, though many grow tall, slender flower stalks. They often have very beautiful leaves, usually basal. In general, the flower structure is like the Rose family, but usually there are as many (or twice as many) stamens as petals. Styles or stigmas are separate, less than the number of petals. The ovaries may be lightly joined and vary in position from partly or wholly inferior to superior, developing into a capsule or berry. The wild species mostly grow on rocky ledges and streambanks. Coral bells are a common garden flower.

Woodland Star, Fringecup, *Lithophragma tenella,* is a white (or pinkish) flower found in shady spots of the mountain 2,000-5,000 feet elevations all over the West. The petals are deeply divided into three to five narrow lobes (resembling the Pink Family, but here the petals are three to five cleft, while Pinks are two cleft or two-by-two cleft). The flowers appear star-like, and are scattered along the slender leafless stem 5-15 inches (12.5-37.5 cm) tall growing from a basal clump of deeply lobed roundish leaves, usually reddish underneath. *Lithophragma affinis* with a V-shaped flower base and *Lithophragma heterophyllum,* U-shaped flower, are the species commonly found in lower elevations.

Bishop's Cap, *Mitella breweri (ovalis),* is a minute, interesting late spring and summer flower. It is usually noticed as a low green carpet along cool streams all over the Northwest, extending into the Rockies. The leaves have scattered white or brown hairs, and are round with a heart-shaped base. The flowering stalk is 6-14 inches (15-35 cm) high, and both it and petioles are covered with soft downward-pointing hairs. The tiny white petals are finely divided and extend beyond the sepals in patterns resembling snowflakes. There are many closely related species.

Alum Root, *Heuchera micrantha,* produces tiny white or pinkish flowers in a loose panicle on a slender stem from a basal clump of leaves. Small narrow petals attached to the wall of the calyx curve over the sepal lobes; the five-lobe calyx is fused to the lower part of the ovary; stamens stand higher than the calyx. The round or ovate leaves are lobed, toothed, and covered with tiny hairs; the petioles and stems have long hairs. Common in the states along the Pacific Coast and in the Sierra and Cascades to 7,000 feet.

STORKSBILL

WHITE-STEMMED FILAREE

LONG-BEAKED FILAREE

CRANESBILL

GERANIUM FAMILY
Geraniaceae

Almost everyone in the world knows geraniums. They grow wild as weeds in Central America. They are kept carefully as potted plants over the long winters in Europe and the eastern United States. In warm climates the garden varieties grow so easily they must be kept pruned to control them, often the prunings will root right on the trash pile. Wild members of the family are filaree, cranesbill, storksbill, and pink geranium. They all have seed pods which are very characteristic — long and slender, developing rapidly after the petals fall off. Five seeds develop in the five-part ovary, each remaining connected to its style (the characteristic long seed pod). When ripe, the five parts separate, each style stays attached to one seed and twists as a corkscrew tail, helping to separate it from the others. There are five sepals, five petals, and five or ten stamens.

Storksbill, Red-stemmed Filaree, Scissors, *Erodium cicutarium,* is known to
most people of the West because it grows over much of the area. The
corkscrew seed pods attach themselves to clothing and animal fur. This is
one way the seeds get scattered. The style begins to grow long as soon as
the petals drop, often becoming 1-1½ inches (2.5-3.8 cm) long. As the
ovary matures, the style splits into its five sections, with one "seed" at
the end of each, then twisting up like a corkscrew. When the ripe seeds
fall to the ground they lie there waiting for moisture. When the corkscrew
gets moist, even with dew, it untwists. As it dries again in the sunshine, it
twists once more, tighter than at first. This way the seed actually screws
itself down into the ground — it plants itself! The flowers are small,
pinkish-purple, four to eight along branching red stems that grow from
rosettes of basal leaves. Blooms over much of the year. Common on
hillsides, fields, and pasturelands. A good food for grazing animals and all
species of filaree are useful for greens, cooked or raw.

White-stemmed Filaree, *Erodium moschatum,* is very similar to the red-
stemmed species except for the stem color.

Long-beaked Filaree, *Erodium botrys*, is another very common species
introduced from Europe which has white hairy stems and very long seed
pods. The flower is deep violet in color on leafy branching stems 6-30
inches (15-75 cm) long. Children make "scissors" out of the seed pods by
thrusting one through the other.

Cranesbill, Pink Geranium, *Geranium incisum,* is one of the most widely
distributed wildflowers of the western mountains. It is very similar to the
wild geranium of the eastern United States and Europe. In the U.S., the
flower is usually white through pale to dark pink or lavendar, ½-1½
inches (1.3-3.9 cm) wide; European species are often pale to deep blue.

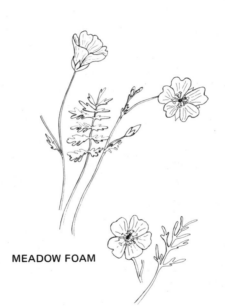

MEADOW FOAM

All have noticeable veins in the petals. The plant grows 12-24 inches (30-60 cm) high with many hairy leafy branches from thick perennial roots. The leaves are palmately divided, many bud stalks developing from each leaf axil. There are ten stamens, each with big anthers, and as the flower matures, five thick stigma tips open. The style grows long as the ovary matures, forming the characteristic "bill;" blooms from May through early August, depending on elevation. The leaves begin to color red by midsummer.

MEADOW FOAM FAMILY
Limnanthaceae

The Meadow Foam Family is very much like the Geranium Family, except it does not have the characteristic long-beaked ovary and long-tailed fruits. The five-part ovary splits into five one-seed nutlets. The leaves are alternate and finely divided. Usually there are five persistent sepals that surround the ovary. Usually there are five petals and twice as many stamens as sepals. Grows in moist fields and meadows.

Meadow Foam, *Limnanthes douglasii,* spreads like white foam over moist valleys and meadows of California and Oregon in March and April. The petals are veined, mostly with yellow; those that grow in the Central Valley of California, *Limnanthes rosea,* usually are veined with pink. The petals often are one inch (2.5 cm) across, wedge-shaped, with a U-shaped band of hairs at the base. The flowers close at night. The leaves are quite succulent, yellowish-green with three to nine toothed divisions. The plants grow 6-14 inches (15-35 cm) high with many smooth brittle branches.

ROSE FAMILY
Rosaceae

A very large and varied family containing herbs, shrubs, and trees, and though there are many variations, all of its members can be recognized fairly easily. The leaves are alternate, often compound, with *stipules*. The calyx is five-parted, in some appearing to be ten-parted because of a row of bractlets attached just below the calyx. Five separate petals, often brightly colored pinks, reds, or yellow, may be fragrant and provide nectar for honey. The stamens are ten (sometimes five) to numerous, inserted, as are the petals, on the calyx, or on the edge of a disc that lines the calyx tube. The few-to-many ovaries may be joined to form a compound pistil with one-to-many styles or stigmas. The ovaries are partly or completely enclosed by the calyx tube. The fruits are various, being achenes,

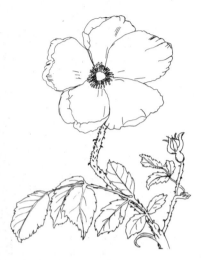

CALIFORNIA WILD ROSE

THIMBLEBERRY

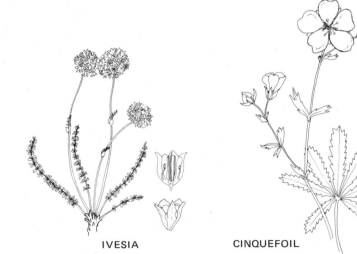

IVESIA

CINQUEFOIL

berries, pods, or pomes. Many of our garden flowers and orchard fruits belong in this family, such as roses, apples, pears, berries. Wild rose is the state flower of Georgia, Iowa, New York, and North Dakota. Rose hips are high in vitamin C: remove the seeds and use the fleshy fruit; make into jellies, dry or freeze.

Wild Rose, *Rosa woodsii* and *Rosa californica,* are two of at least 100 wild roses found all over the world. All are very similar and are easily recognized as members of this family, but are individually often hard to distinguish. The dainty pink flowers grow in clusters, each having five sepals, five petals, many stamens and pistils. The receptacle grows urn-shaped and holds the pistils as the fleshy fruit matures. The fruits often color in the fall. Many birds feed on these "rose hips" and they were gathered and dried for food by the Indians. Since they are high in vitamin C they were also used by the British during World War II to supplement their diets. *Rosa woodsii* is the Rocky Mountain rose from Canada to New Mexico. *Rosa californica* is common in Oregon and California.

Thimbleberry, Salmonberry, *Rubus parviflorus,* is common all over the West and as far east as Michigan. It grows in woods and mountains and is recognizable mostly by the five-lobed enormous leaves, 2-8 inches (5-20 cm), shiny green above, gray-green below. The white flower is 1-2 inches (2.5-5 cm) across with three to six flowers in a group. The fruit looks like a luscious raspberry, but has little flavor and blooms from spring to midsummer; the tender shoots are also edible.

Ivesia, *Ivesia gordonii,* is a common plant, blooming from late June into August on semi dry to moist rocky slopes from 7,000 feet to above timberline in the Sierra and Rockies. It has small yellow flowers in tight clusters on unbranched stalks 2-10 inches (5-25 cm) high from a dense leafy clump. The leaves seem fern-like or like a slim tail, 2-6 inches (5-15 cm) long. The flower clusters appear parchment-like because the dry yellowish calyx grow larger as the petals wither. This flower some- what resembles yarrow in the Composite Family.

Cinquefoil, Five-fingers, Potentilla, *Potentilla gracilis,* is a common yellow flower with many varieties and many relatives, but the genus can be recognized by several features. The five sepals are triangular, with the tip just showing between the petals, and in between each two is a narrow bract, so it looks as though there are ten sepals. Flowers are ½ inch (1.3 cm) wide, the white ones are like strawberry blossoms and the yellow species might be mistaken for buttercups, but these do not have shiny petals. The leaves are very characteristic; they are compound and each leaflet is toothed. This species has five to seven leaflets palmately arranged (hence the name), with most leaves basal with long petioles. Other species have pinnately arranged leaflets five to twenty in number, such as *Potentilla glandulosa,* a common pale yellow species over most of

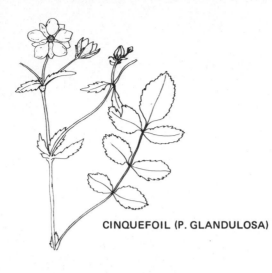

CINQUEFOIL (P. GLANDULOSA)

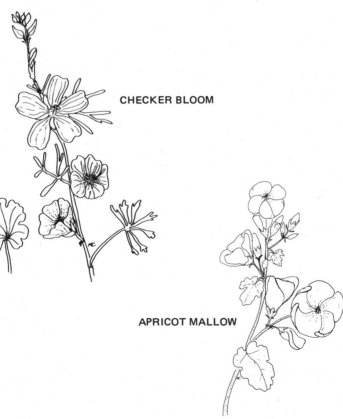

CHECKER BLOOM

APRICOT MALLOW

the West and extending east of the Rockies. The basal leaves in this species have seven to nine leaflets, upper ones usually have three leaflets.

There are numerous stamens, and many achenes are produced—again a characteristic of this genus, since most members of the Rose Family produce a fleshy fruit. Potentillas grow in meadows and woods, from low margins of the deserts and plains to 8,000 feet. Found from Alaska to California and throughout the Rocky Mountains; the Arctic potentilla also grows in Siberia.

MALLOW FAMILY
Malvaceae

This is a large family found over much of the world. The most easily recognized characteristic is the collar or column of many stamens with their filaments all united, surrounding the compound pistil. The claws of the five petals are united to the base of this column. There are five sepals, but often there is a row of bracts below them, so it looks as though there are ten sepals. The five petals twist in the bud. The mature ovary in many species looks like a flat cheese, giving the common name of cheese weed to some of its members. The ovary splits apart into kidney-shaped sections, as does an orange. Most Mallows have perfect flowers, but some have separate staminate and pistillate flowers, some have staminate and pistillate plants. They are mostly herbs, but some are shrubs and all have a sticky, stringy juice. The inner bark is tough and fibrous. The leaves are alternate, simple, palmately veined and lobed, and often very beautiful. Both leaves and stems may be hairy. Many have beautiful flowers. Hollyhocks and hibiscus are favorite garden Mallows, Marshmallows, in the early days, were made from the sticky juices of a Mallow that grew in the marshes. Cotton and okra are important commercial members of this family.

Checker Bloom, *Sidalcea malvaeflora,* is a common pink flower found among the grasses of California and Oregon roadsides and fields. The five notched petals are noticeably veined, with smooth, white bases; blooms April to June.

Apricot Mallow, *Sphaeralcea ambigus,* is a summer-blooming Mallow of California, Nevada, Utah, Idaho, and Arizona, found from 2,000–6,000 feet elevations. The salmon-colored flowers are scattered thickly along the top part of the stem. The yellow center and yellow stamen column seem to give it a yellow "eye." Flowers usually ½ inch (1.3 cm) across, though they vary with rainfall. The leaves are gray, fuzzy, fairly thick, and are shallowly three-lobed with many folds and frills to the margin.

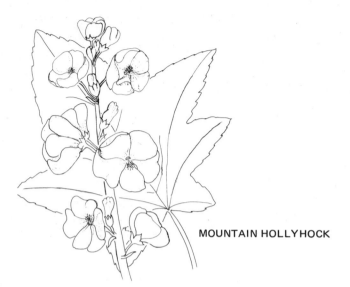

MOUNTAIN HOLLYHOCK

KLAMATH WEED

Scarlet Globemallow, *Sphaeralcea coccinea,* is similar to apricot mallow except for the brick-red color. It is common on the prairie and plains of the country, and in the lower, drier areas of the Rocky Mountains. It was eaten as greens by the Indians.

Mountain Hollyhock, Stream Globemallow, *Iliamus (Sphaeralcea) rivularis* is a 3-6 feet (90-180 cm), stout, many branched plant found along roadsides, streams, and wherever the soil is rich and moist, from low hills to 9,000 feet over the Northwest, Canada, California, Nevada, and Colorado. Flowers are soft pink to deep pink in dense spikes, 1-2 inches across. Leaves are 2-6 inches (5-15 cm) across, with three to seven toothed lobes.

ST. JOHN'S-WORT FAMILY
Hypericaceae

The flowers in this family are bright yellow with persistent sepals and long stamens sometimes arranged in groups. The ovary is one-to-three-celled, with three styles, and develops into a capsule. The opposite leaves and branches have tiny black or clear dots scattered all along.

Klamath Weed, Goatweed, St. John's-Wort, *Hypericum perforatum,* has bright yellow flowers ¾-1 inch (1.9-2.5 cm) wide, which grow in clusters at ends of the many opposite branches. The petals have tiny black dots along the edges or scattered over the surface. The plant grows 1-5 feet (30-150 cm) tall from a woody branching rootstock, blooming from May to September in pastures, fields, and open woods over much of the West from low elevations to 5,000 feet. It is an introduced weed from Europe and has completely taken over vast pasturelands. A beetle which feeds on this plant has been brought in and is doing a fair control job.

OXALIS FAMILY
Oxalidaceae

These are small plants with sour juice and palmately compound leaves with theee leaflets. Plants often are called "sour clover" by children because of this juice and leaf shape; used in salads. The leaves fold and droop at night. The flowers are built on the plan of five with five sepals, five petals, ten stamens (usually in two rows with their filaments united at the base) and a superior five-cell ovary with five styles. The capsule is many-seeded. Most of the family are tropical plants, but there are a few species in the West. One of the most common is a small weed introduced from Europe, especially

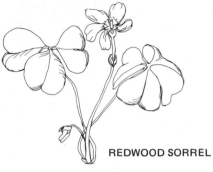

REDWOOD SORREL

LITTLE YELLOW SORREL

BLUE FLAX

found in gardens of the Southwest. Some species of Oxalis produce runners, and one bright yellow species has invaded orchards of California. It produces many small bulbs.

Wood Sorrel, Redwood Sorrel, *Oxalis oregana,* is a small woods plant with clover-like leaves, but flowers not at all clover-like. They form clumps about 6 inches (15 cm) tall, growing from a creeping rootstock. Each palmately compound leaf grows singly at the end of a slender, hairy, petiole, the leaflets usually having a lighter spot of green showing on the surface. The flowers grow singly on stalks with a pair of tiny bracts near the top. The 1-1½ inch (2.5-3.8 cm) flowers may be white, pink, or rose, shading to yellow at the base. The petals appear very delicate, and usually are veined with pink. This attractive plant is grown in gardens, both for the foliage and flowers. It blooms in spring along the coastal regions of northern California, Oregon, and Washington.

Little Yellow Sorrel, *Oxalis corniculata,* is a common garden weed. Leaves, stems, and flowers may be tinged with purple, making the plant appear bronzed. It is abundant over the Southwest, blooming from spring to fall.

FLAX FAMILY
Linaceae

This family has been known and used by man since ancient times; linen is made from the stem fiber and linseed oil from the seed. There are annual or perennial species with small narrow alternate, or sometimes opposite, leaves growing more or less along all stems. The flowers are blue with a few species being yellow or white. They grow in panicles, are built on the plan of five with five sepals, five separate petals that fall early, five stamens at least partly fused at their bases, and a superior, several-celled ovary with as many (or twice as many) cells as there are styles; styles are separate, not united. The fruit is a capsule with oily seeds.

Blue Flax, *Linum lewisii,* is the common blue flax of the West. It is a perennial plant with several straight thin upright stems from a woody base. The 1-3 foot (30-90 cm) tall stems have many small narrow bluish-green leaves, the flowers in loose clusters at the top. The lovely soft blue, saucer-shaped, veined petals often are an inch (2.5 cm) across. They fall soon after blooming, but the sepals are persistent. The little round capsule has ten valves. It grows particularly well on drier slopes and ridges from low elevations to 9,000 feet from Alaska south throughout the West to Mexico.

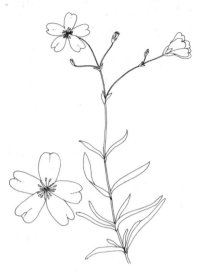

FIELD CHICKWEED

COMMON CHICKWEED

WINDMILL PINK

PINK FAMILY
Caryophyllaceae

A family of small plants, many form mats of color, but must not be confused with the Phlox Family that has united petals. The leaves are simple and are always opposite. The flower is on the plan of five (sometimes four), perfect and regular with five (four) sepals that persist. The sepals may be separate or fused into a tubular calyx. In some species, this tubular calyx becomes enlarged and vase-shaped. The petals are often notched (or cleft at the tip, sometimes doubly so). The stamens are the same number (or double) as the petals. There are one to five styles, but the superior ovary is just one-celled. Seeds are in a capsule or achene. Pinks and carnations are garden flowers; many varieties, including double ones, have been developed.

Field Chickweed, *Cerastium arvense,* is often found in dense masses of white bloom in the mountains of the world. It may also grow as separate little clumps in meadows and mountain slopes, both dry and moist spots. It grows from a perennial rootstock. It is particularly noticed because its five petals are deeply notched and the stems are strong enough so the plant stands up among the grasses. The five sepals are separate, the five notched petals ¼-½ inch (.6-1.3 cm) across and at least twice the size of the sepals. The stems and opposite leaves are somewhat fuzzy. The leaves are mostly basal. Chickweed blooms from April to September, depending on location, altitude, and moisture; Alaska to California, across the United States and Eurasia.

Common Chickweed, *Stellaria media*   The scientific name comes from the perfect five point star shape of the sepals alternating with the five deeply notched petals; little low, weak-stemmed, somewhat succulent plant that is an introduced weed from Europe now found along moist spots, fences, gardens, and in lawns. The five white deeply notched petals are tiny, the sepals longer than petals. The stamens are tiny and vary in number. Use tender stems in salad or cook for greens or soup seasoning.

Windmill Pink, *Silene gallica,* is a drab weed of the roadsides of the Northwest, but it is common and shows the characteristics of this family. The slender, hairy stem often is branched and about 12 inches (30 cm) high. Flowers tend to bloom on just one side of the stalk. Leaves are simple, opposite, and hairy. The calyx is the noticeable flower part. It is tan-purplish, hairy, sticky, and vase-shaped. The dull white or pinkish petals are "twisted" like the arms of a windmill. Each petal has a small scale where the blade of the petal joins the claw, forming a small "crown" at the top of the throat. This weed came from Europe, but is now found in most places of the temperate zone of the world, beginning to bloom in April and May in the Northwest.

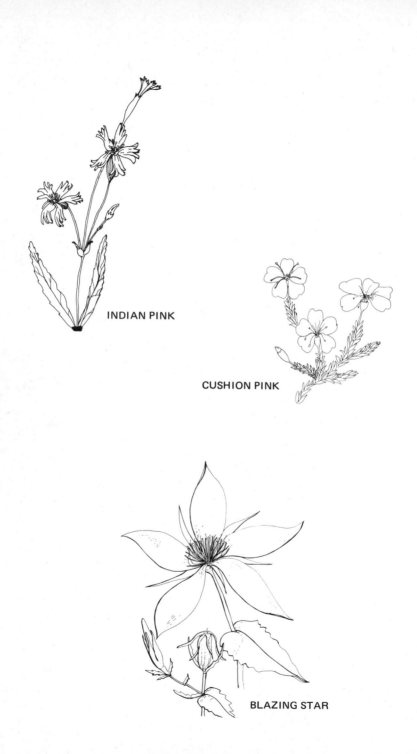

INDIAN PINK

CUSHION PINK

BLAZING STAR

Indian Pink, *Silene californica,* is a fabulous crimson flower 1-2 inches (2.5-5 cm) across with the blade of the five petals deeply divided in fours. Two very noticeable scales on the inside of each petal tip inward in a "crown" where the long claw joins the expanded blade. The ten stamens stand stiffly above the petals; the stigma is three-parted. The 6-12 inch (15-30 cm) tall, slender, leafy stem from a long tap root produces two or three blossoms at the ends. The clasping, opposite, gray-green leaves are up to 3 inches (2.5 cm) long and downy with soft hairs. The flowers make a brilliant splash of color and are widely distributed in the Northwest, though never abundantly common. A similar flower, *Silene laciniata,* is very common in southern California. This species has rough, sticky leaves and stems.

Cushion Pink, Moss Campion, *Silene acaulis,* is a high mountain pink that makes a tight mat of tiny, stiff, green leaves covered with pink-purple flowers. The bell-shaped calyx holds the five-petaled small flowers, each with a "crown" of scales between claw and blade. It resembles creeping phlox in general growth and appearance, but the petals are separate. It blooms in high mountain areas up to 13,000 feet across the United States, Canada, Europe and Asia.

LOASA FAMILY (EVENING STAR FAMILY)
Loasaceae

This is an American family which has brilliant flowers usually with many stamens (ten to one hundred-fifty). Both the hard stems and prickly leaves may be whitish and covered with barbed or hooked hairs. The flowers have five sepal-lobes and five petals. The numerous filaments are thread-like; sometimes five outer ones are much broader and petal-like. The style, which may be divided at the tip, is also thread-like. The one-celled inferior ovary forms a capsule that opens between the persistent calyx lobes at the tip. Many species open in late afternoon and close in the morning. The petals are luminescent and can be seen in the dark, the flowers resembling cactus.

Blazing Star, Stickleaf, *Mentzelia laevicaulis,* has beautiful shiny pale lemon-yellow flowers in clusters of two or three at the end of stiff branches. The plant is 2-3½ feet (60-105 cm) high with shiny, almost white, stems. The leaves are lance-shaped, toothed, 3-7 inches (7.5-17.5 cm) long, covered with barbed hairs. These make the brittle plant parts stick to clothing or animals (or prevent their being picked or eaten). Each flower may be 2-4 inches (5-10 cm) across. The five outer stamens (there are many) have wide filaments and appear petal-like. This plant is found on dry slopes, road cuts, dry streambeds, etc. from foothills to 6,000 feet, California and Oregon, east to the Rockies and throughout the Great Basin

FOOTSTEPS OF SPRING

area to northern Arizona. Blooms from mid-June to late August. It is a very striking plant and may grow in masses. Other species of *Mentzelia* which grow in the West are very similar. Indians ground the seeds of some species (especially *Mentzelia albicaulis*) for flour.

PARSLEY or CARROT FAMILY
Umbelliferae

The Umbelliferae Family was given its name because the tiny flowers are arranged in umbels ("umbrella" comes from the same Latin word), often with umbels within the main umbel, making a very big lacy arrangement. The umbel is surrounded by petal-like bracts, some of them quite large. The flowers of all the family are so much alike that the different groups are identified by the fruit, which is dry and seed-like. The fruit is of two parts, with the seeds face to face, and the backs having various ribs, wings, prickles, hairs, and oil tube arrangements. The small oil tubes make many of them strong-smelling. The stems of most are hollow; some of them grow very tall, up to 8 feet (2.4 m). The leaves are alternate or basal, and usually finely divided. The umbels dry persistent, and may be used for winter decoration. Many plants of this family have been used since ancient times as food or seasonings. The roots of carrots and parsnips, the leaves or stems of parsley and celery, and the seeds of anise and caraway are examples. The early colonists in Massachusetts and Virginia planted carrots as one of their main foods. Some of the *Umbelliferae,* however, are poisonous, or have poisonous parts. The "hemlock cup" of the ancient Greeks was made from a member of this family; the leaves of some are poisonous to grazing animals; some members have parts useful in medicine. However, there are so many poisonous species that *no wild member of this family should be eaten unless the identification is positive.*

Footsteps of Spring, *Sanicula arctopoides,* is well-named, for it is one of the first flowers to bloom, making greenish-yellow mats of color on the hillsides as grass is just beginning to show. The many toothed yellow-green leaves are basal, the umbels on short stems. The umbel is made of tiny yellow flowers, surrounded by conspicuous yellow-green petal-like bracts. Some of the flowers have no pistil. Found from central California to Canada, they bloom from January through March.

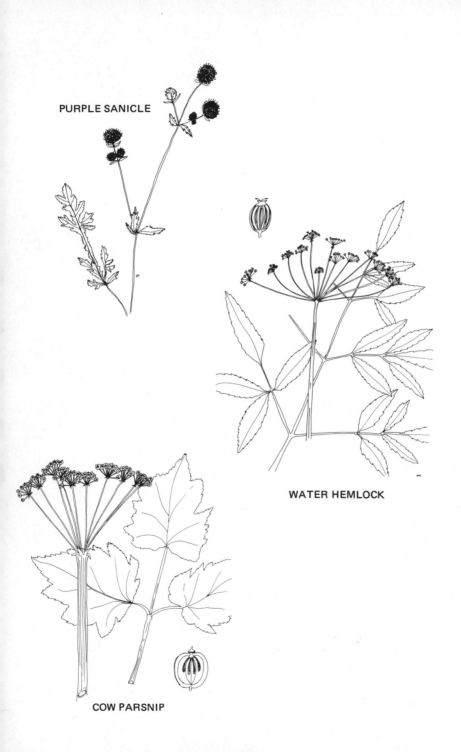

PURPLE SANICLE

WATER HEMLOCK

COW PARSNIP

Purple Sanicle, *Sanicula bipinnatifida*   The umbels of this dull purple-red flower (there is a yellow variety) are crowded together to make tiny balls less than ½ inch (1.3 cm) in diameter. The stamens are long and suggest pins sticking in a pincushion. The smooth, dark green to purple leaves are finely divided into three, five, or seven beautiful lobed or toothed parts. The plant grows ½-1 foot (15-30 cm) high, blooming early in the spring, often with blue dicks, in grassy fields and hillsides in coastal areas and Sierran foothills in California, north to Canada, from March to May.

Water Hemlock, *Cicuta douglasii*   A very poisonous member of this family, found all over the West, California to Alaska, east to Alberta and the Rockies, south to Arizona and New Mexico. It grows along streams from low altitudes to 8,000 feet. Cows and other large animals are quickly killed from eating the leaves. The white flowers are small, growing in compound umbels which are not flat topped. Usually there is no bract at the base of the umbel, or if any, it is small. The plant is often tall, but may be any where from 2-6 feet (60-180 cm). Stiff stems grow from thick tubers; leaves, stems, and tubers are poisonous, with the tubers the most poisonous. The leaves may be slightly purplish and are 6-16 inches (15-40 cm) long, double pinnately compound with edges like saw teeth. The leaf veins end at notches rather than tips of teeth as is the usual pattern in leaves. The ''seeds'' have light colored corky ribs, but no wings or hooks.

Cow Parsnip, *Heracleum lanatum*, is a large, tall, big-leafed perennial member of the Parsley Family. The large leaf is one of its best characteristics; it usually has three toothed and lobed leaflets, each 4-10 inches (10-25 cm) wide. The stems are hairy and the plant grows 3-6 feet (90-180 cm) tall, capped by big flat compound umbels. These may be as wide as 1 foot (30 cm)! The flowers are white, the outer flowers having larger petals than the inner ones. It is abundant from low altitudes to 8,000 feet, along streams, meadow edges or open woods over most of North America; also common in Asia, blooming early in the summer. The ''seeds'' are rounded, but flattened sideways, ⅓ inch (.8 cm) long with oil tubes halfway down the sides.

It is used in some of the Blackfoot Indian ceremonies; Northwest Indians ate the young shoots though the stems (if not peeled) and the leaves may raise blisters when touched. The foliage has been reported as poisonous to cattle.

HEATH FAMILY (*now* including WINTERGREEN FAMILY)
Ericaceae

This is a fairly large family, including trees (madrone, kalmia), shrubs (azaleas, rhododendrons, manzanita), low evergreen creeping shrubs (mountain heather), perennial evergreen herbs (prince's pine

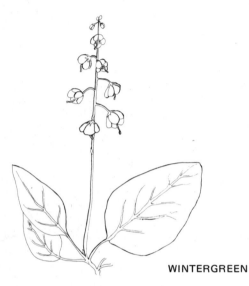

WINTERGREEN

PRINCE'S PINE

and wintergreen), and plants which have no green parts (snow plant). The plants with no green parts are saprophytes, whose roots grow in close association with fungi, which break down forest humus into a form that dependent plants can use. Saprophytes vary in color from white through brown to brilliant red. The flowers usually grow in a spike or raceme, often with a similarly colored bract below each flower. Most botanists now include the Wintergreen (*Pyrola*) Family in the Heath Family.

There are five (rarely four) petals and sepals. The petals may be separate (prince's pine and wintergreen), partly united (azaleas), or completely united into vase-shaped flowers (heathers). The lower petal in some may be somewhat larger and more highly colored. Flowers may be red, pinkish, or white with five to ten stamens. The calyx is persistent. The ovary, usually five-celled, and superior, has a long persistent style. The fruit may be a berry (blueberry, cran berry), but most Heaths produce a capsule with a hard outer surface. This capsule, split into five parts, often persists, standing or hanging from its stem through the winter months. Many are useful for dried arrangements. Usually grows in mountainous areas over much of North America, Europe, and Asia.

Wintergreen, White-veined Shinleaf, *Pyrola picta,* is low-growing with creeping rootstocks. The leafless flower stalk grows from a cluster of basal leaves which are often shiny. Some species have round leaves, others are oval and up to 2½ inches (6.3 cm) long. The white-veined shinleaf has noticeable white leaf veins or spots and each flower stalk has ten to twenty small hanging greenish or tannish flowers. The lowest petal is larger than the others. The ten stamens turn toward the upper petals; the style bends down towards the largest petal, and then turns outwards. Wintergreen grows in cool forested areas from 4,000-6,000 feet. It is found in all the mountains of the West. *Pyrola asarifolia* has succulent or waxy white petals with pink edges looking like apple blossoms. Other species are common in the Appalachians.

Prince's Pine, Pipsissewa, *Chimaphila umbellata*   This beautiful little evergreen plant has clusters of waxy-petaled hanging flowers on pinkish stems above the narrow leathery dark green leaves. The finely toothed leaves, 1-2½ inches (2.5-6.3 cm) long, are arranged in whorls or clusters on the stems, not basal as in most wintergreens. The petals are pink to white, each concave and standing outwards, showing off the ten stamens with dilated hairy filaments. Found in moist pine woods and along streams from 100 to 6,000 feet in the Coast Ranges and Sierra, north to Alaska, in the Rockies, mountains of eastern United States, in Europe and Asia.

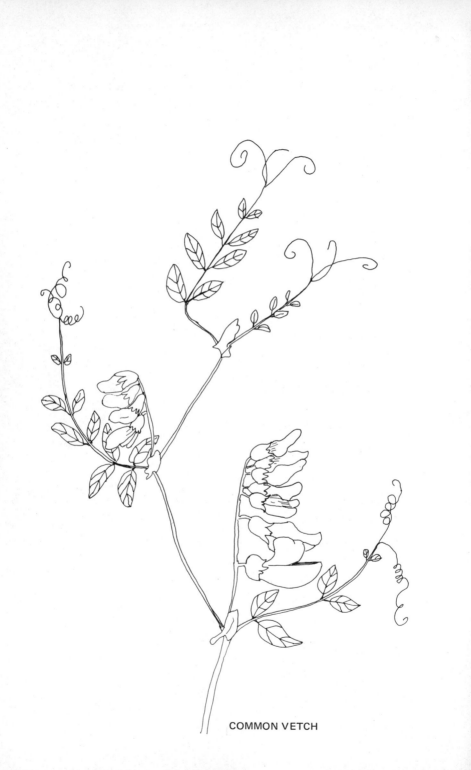

COMMON VETCH

Chapter VII

FIVE SEPARATE PETALS
NOT ALL ALIKE

Members of this group are common garden flowers, so they are familiar to all. They include the large Pea Family, the Violet Family, and a few irregularly shaped flowers of the Buttercup Family.

PEA FAMILY
Leguminosae

This family has many wildflowers, of many sizes and colors, some even grow as shrubs and trees. The shape of the petals is very characteristic. The large upper one is called the "standard" or "banner," and covers the others in the bud; two side petals are called "wings," the bottom petal is called a "keel," but really it is two petals, lightly joined. Hiding inside the keel are the ten stamens. Often nine stamens, sometimes all ten, have united filaments, making a collar around the ovary and curved style. The superior ovary is one-celled; the pod is two-sided, with many seeds (peas and beans are excellent examples). This pod is called a legume, and is characteristic of *all* the family. Common members for food are: peas, beans, licorice for humans; alfalfa, clover, and vetch for animals. Acacia, redbud, and mesquite are examples of trees that belong to this family. Although we have many edible legumes, lupines should be avoided, particularly the seeds, for they have a higher concentration of poison.

Vetch, *Vicia sativa,* is a low growing, vine-like plant with angular stems. The stems have many pinnately compound leaves and end in tendrils. The flowers grow on a one-sided raceme. The edges of the purple banner turn back, and the red wings fit over the middle of the pink keel. The calyx is a tube with five teeth, the fruit is a flat pod. Vetches of many species grow all over America and Europe, and all species resemble one another very closely. Vetch is useful as a cover crop in orchards; it is plowed into the soil as a fertilizer because it produces so much nitrogen. It also is a valuable food for cattle, horses, and sheep.

ANNUAL or DOVE LUPINE

Lupinus succulentus

DESERT LUPINE

Lupinus pusillus

LUPINES or BLUEBONNETS are members of the Pea Family and are among the best known of spring wildflowers. They grow in great colorful masses, often with California poppies, paintbrushes, columbines, etc., depending on the area. There are many species and varieties of different sizes, shapes, and colors; often it is hard to tell species apart. All lupines have palmately compound leaves with five to many leaflets and the flowers grow in whorls on the stem. Both the leaves and the stems were used as food by the Indians who also used the seeds for a medicinal tea, however, they do contain poison and all species should be avoided. The Texas bluebonnet, *Lupinus subcarnosus,* is the state flower of Texas; garden varieties have been developed.

Annual or Dove Lupine, *Lupinus bicolor,* is a common early small blue and white lupine that spills masses of color on the grassy hills of the coast from mid California north to Vancouver; it is less common in the Sierran foothills. The sides of the banner are turned upwards and the keel is slender. The soft hairy plant may be 4-16 inches (10-40 cm) tall with few flowers on each stalk. Also blooming in March and April is the taller, up to 24 inches (60 cm), *Lupinus nanus,* sky lupine, which grows on grassy coastal and Sierran valley and hills. All the petals are broad (not turned backwards). The banner has a yellow or white center with blue dots. The yellow or white of both species may change to reddish or violet as the flower ages. Both species have five to seven leaflets.

Lupinus succulentus is the most common annual lupine of the foothills of the Coast Ranges and Sierra. It is widespread in southern and Lower California and east onto the prairies in the central part of the country. The succulent, branching plant grows 8-24 inches (20-60 cm) high, with leaves of seven to nine leaflets with a long petiole. The flower is a dark blue to almost white, with a yellow spot on the banner which later turns purple; both wings and keel have hairy bases. It blooms in ravines, moist hillsides and along roadsides in February and March. It is coarser and the plants are bigger than *Lupinus bicolor* or *Lupinus nanus* and doesn't produce the color mass.

Desert Lupine, *Lupinus odoratus,* is a low lupine with long-petioled basal leaves. The blue or purple flowers are scattered along the spike; the banner has a yellow center and the keel is slightly curved. Grows in sandy areas of southern California, east into Nevada and Arizona.

Lupinus pusillus is a very widespread, small annual lupine with five leaflets. The long petiole stands higher than the flower racemes. The flowers are blue to whitish, with a straight keel, and are not whorled on the stem. The pod produces just two seeds. It is common in dry sandy soil throughout the West.

Lupinus torreyi

YELLOW OR BUSH LUPINE

LOCO WEED

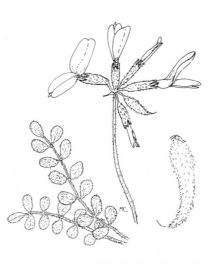

SCARLET LOCOWEED

Lupinus torreyi is a lupine covered with flat-lying hairs. The leaves are long-petioled with six to eight leaflets. The flower racemes stand above the leaf clump and bear many tightly grouped violet-blue flowers. The banner is not hairy, and changes from yellow to purple with age. The keel is slightly curved and is hairy on the upper edge; the wings are longer than the banner. Found in the well-drained areas of the Sierra, north into eastern Washington, usually in soils formed from granitic rocks.

Lupinus sericeus, a blue or blue-lavender lupine and the taller, though not as big-flowered, lodge pole lupine, *Lupinus parviflorus,* are the common lupines of the Rocky Mountains. The dense flower racemes are at the ends of leafy branches 1-2 feet (30-60 cm) tall. They grow in mountains and valleys of the Rockies to 7,000 feet.

Yellow or Bush Lupine, *Lupinus arboreus*   This gorgeous yellow perennial lupine may grow to be a woody shrub producing dozens of big, 6-12 inches (15-30 cm), spikes of bright yellow fragrant blossoms. It commonly grows near the coast and in the canyons of California; in some areas it may be bluish. There are six to eleven blue-green leaflets on a short petiole, downy on the underside. An easily recognized plant, and as with many lupines, quite readily grown from seed.

Loco Weed, Balloon Plant, Rattle Weed, *Astragalus nuttalii*   This very large group of plants in the Pea Family is found from low dry hot desert areas to high mountain spots. The many species closely resemble each other and are difficult to tell apart. The number of flowers and leaflets and the characteristics of the pods are some of the features used to distinguish the species. The plants branch profusely, have pinnately compound leaves, and the leaflets are often densely hairy. The flowers resemble vetch, but the seed pods may become enlarged and parchement like, often very colorful, or densely woolly or crescent-shaped.

   Astragalus nuttalii (menziesii) is a common coastal species which produces clusters of large inflated seed pods 1½-2 inches (3.8-5 cm) long, resembling groups of small ballons. The many, twenty to forty, gray to dark green leaflets are hairy; the abundant, twenty to ninety, greenish-white, ½ inch (1.3 cm) flowers with pale yellow-green calyxes are clustered together in dense racemes 3-6 inches (7.5-15 cm) long. Grows in sandy soils near the coast from San Francisco south.

   Astralagus pomonensis is very similar with twenty-five to forty-one leaflets, petals greenish white or yellowish, with inflated papery pods. Grows along coastal California from San Luis Obispo to Lower California and in the interior valleys of southern California.

Scarlet Locoweed, Crimson Woolly Pod, *Astralagus coccineus,* is a fabulous desert species. This silvery gray plant forms low clumps 6-10 inches (15-25 cm) across, with many bright red flowers an inch (2.5 cm) or more in length. The pods are even longer and densely woolly. Grows in canyon's

BUR CLOVER

TOMCAT CLOVER

114

and gravelly ridges 2,100-7,000 feet from Owens Valley and Death Valley to Lower California and east into Arizona.

Some species of locoweed absorb enough of the mineral silenium from shale soils to poison animals, giving them "loco" disease.

Bur Clover, *Medicago hispida,* is both a pest (in lawns and gardens) and a valuable plant as a nutritious food for cattle, horses, and sheep, and a valuable cover crop for orchards. It is a common wildflower, its little blossoms making bright patches of yellow or orange. The plants grow in masses on plains and low hills all over America. It grows flat on the ground, with long-spreading creeping stems from the taproot. The seed pods twist so tightly in spirals they form little flat balls. Since these are bordered with a double row of sharp little hooked prickles, they form a "bur." This is another European plant which has traveled to America and Australia.

Tomcat Clover, Trefoil, *Trifolium tridentatum,* is one of the most common clovers from Canada to California along the Pacific Ocean, growing from the coast through fields, valleys and hillsides to about 4,000 feet in the mountains. It is abundant and shows many variations according to its habitat. The plant produces many spreading stems 4-20 inches (10-62.5 cm) long. Each leaf is divided into three leaflets (scientific name shows this), which may have smooth or finely toothed margins. The flowers grow in a round head, each flower standing out separately. The banner is folded and the wings stand at right angles. Corolla is purple, often ranging from dull to bright, and each flower is surrounded by a toothed involucre. It produces a typical pod.

VIOLET FAMILY
Violaceae

Violets are known by everyone; three hundred species of wild violets grow all over the world. They may be blue, lavender, white, yellow, or a combination. Most of the seeds are produced late in the season by special flowers close to the ground (or even under it). Often those late flowers have no petals and are self-pollinated.

There are five sepals which persist, protecting the capsule. The five petals are "irregular," with two upper ones alike, two side ones alike, and one lower petal with a spur or nectar sac at its base. The five stamens with short, broad filaments are placed tightly over the plump, ten-cell ovary. The walls of the ripe ovary curl open into three parts with such force that the seeds are popped out several feet; also grows from perennial rootstocks. Violets and pansies are favorite garden plants. Violets are state flowers for Illinois, Rhode Island, Wisconsin and New Jersey.

PURPLE VIOLET

JOHNNY—JUMP—UP

YELLOW VIOLET

MONKSHOOD

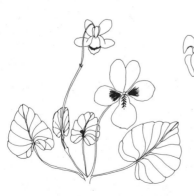

WESTERN HEART'S EASE

Viola adunca is the common violet of North America. The violet to blue flowers grow from a tight low perennial clump of many small shiny round-ovate leaves. The two side petals are very fuzzy at the throat, and the lower petals have some purple veining. The spur is about the length of the upper petals. Blooms over a long period of time on rock ledges, along streams and moist places in shade.

Johnny-Jump-Up, Yellow Pansy-Violet, *Viola pedunculata,* is the bright yellow violet that grows in sunny spots on the grassy hills of California from April to June. The two upper petals are brownish on the back, other petals are purple-veined in the center. The sepals are not all the same size, and each has an ear-like part at the base. The plants are 4-13 inches (10-32.5 cm) high, growing from thick rootstocks. The leaves were eaten as greens by the California Indians. (Cover photograph.)

Yellow Violet, *Viola nuttallii*   This common bright yellow mountain violet is recognized by the short brown veins on the lower petal. The leaves are lance-shaped, slightly toothed and often taller than the flowers. The plants grow 2-7 inches (5-17.5 cm) high, depending on the amount of shade. Found on dry slopes, pine woods, and meadows, 2,000-7,000 feet, from central California north to British Columbia and east through the Rockies.

Western Heart's Ease, Redwood Violet, *Viola ocellata,* is a bicolored violet, with the two upper petals white on the inside but purple outside, the side petals yellowish (or white) with a deep purple spot on each, and the lower petal yellowish (or white) with purple veins in the throat. Basal leaves are 1-2½ inches (2.5-6.3 cm) long, heart or triangular-shaped. The leaves on the many branching flower stems are the same shape, but smaller. Blooms from March to June in shady woods, particularly in moist woods such as redwood areas, from central coastal California north through Oregon.

BUTTERCUP FAMILY
Ranunculaceae

Monkshood, *Aconitum columbianum,* is a member of the Buttercup Family but its petals are so different it fits into this chapter. It has five separate petals, but the two upper ones are small and hidden under one of the sepals which is colored like a petal and arches up to form a "hood." These two petals have spurs and claws. The three lower petals are very small, sometimes missing entirely. Under the hood are the many stamens surrounding the mound of three to five separate pistils (which is characteristic of the Buttercups). The flowers are bright blue, or lavender, tinged with white, veined with purple. They grow on plants 6-8 feet (180-240 cm) tall, with deeply divided leaves, in moist mountain meadows or along streams. Found all over the West from British Columbia south in mountainous areas, 4,000-8,000 feet elevation. Several species grow in the East.

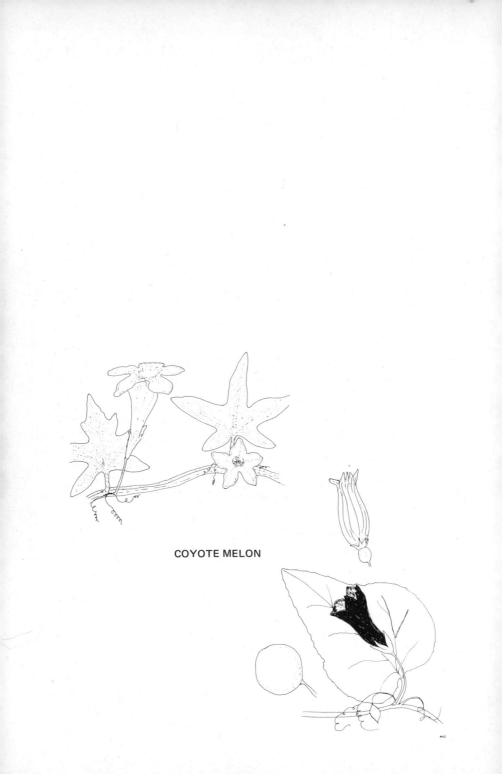

COYOTE MELON

Chapter VIII

FIVE UNITED PETALS ALL ALIKE

A very large group of flowers has five united petals which are all alike. Often the petals are united only at the base, but many have petals that are bell- or even funnel-shaped. Some have distinct petal lobes, others are so united they appear as a single circular petal; all have lines or markings which show they have five petals which are united.

CUCUMBER or GOURD FAMILY
Cucurbitaceae

These are trailing vines, usually with tendrils, often with large palmately veined and lobed leaves. The plants have two kinds of flowers, each with lobed corollas. The staminate flower has only three stamens; pistillate flower has an inferior, one- to six-cell ovary, and two or three stigmas. The calyx lobes usually are narrow and united to the inferior ovary in the pistillate flower. This ovary becomes large, often fleshy (pumpkins) or may become dry (gourds). Squash and cucumbers are also members.

Gourd, Coyote Melon, Calabazilla, *Cucurbita foetidissima, Cucurbita palmata,* are large rank vines with big gray-green hairy or sand-papery leaves that give off a very unpleasant odor when crushed. The large, 2-3 inches (5-7.5 cm), yellow flowers are trumpet-shaped. The vines may be 15-25 feet (4.5-7.5m) in length. Fruits are hard-shelled, smooth, striped, 3 inches (7.5 cm) in diameter. They grow abundantly in central and southern California and in the deserts of Arizona and Texas. *Cucurbita foetidissima* has large triangular leaves and a three-celled fruit; *Cucurbita palmata* has palmately divided leaves, heavily ribbed stems and a five-celled fruit.

WILD CUCUMBER

WHITE MOUNTAIN HEATHER

Wild Cucumber, Common Man Root, Chilicothe, *Echinocystis (Marah) fabacea*   This trailing vine may be as long as 30 feet (9m). It has beautiful, grape-like, palmately-lobed and veined leaves, 1-4 inches (2-10 cm) wide. There are many tendrils. The flowers are star-shaped, greenish cream, and less than ¼ inch (.7 cm) wide. On the same plant there may be both five- and six-lobed flowers. The numerous staminate flowers are noticeable because they grow in branching racemes 3-6 inches (7.5-15cm) long. Pistillate flowers are solitary, growing on short pedicels in the leaf axils. There are many groups of staminate flowers and several scattered pistillate flowers along the vine, with the round spiny inferior ovaries of the older flowers quite mature while buds are still developing at the growing tip. The mature, spiny, fleshy ovary, 2-3 inches (5-7.5 cm) across, is usually four-seeded. The seeds are so round they were used as marbles and in games by Spanish children; they were called Chilicothe beans. The vine trails on the ground or over bushes and trees on California hillsides, in chaparral areas and woods. The root is enormous. The related species, *Echinocystis oreganus,* from San Francisco north into Oregon, is similar, with white flowers.

HEATH FAMILY including WINTERGREEN FAMILY
Ericaceae

This is a fairly large family, including trees (madrone and kalmia), shrubs (azalea and rhododendron), low evergreen creeping shrubs (mountain heather), perennial evergreen herbs (wintergreen and prince's pine), and plants with no green parts (snow plant). The plants with no green parts are saprophytes, whose roots grow in close association with fungi which break down forest humus into a form that dependent plants can use. Saprophytes often grow rapidly when conditions are just right, similar to mushroom growth. The saprophytes vary in color from white through brown to brilliant red. The flowers usually grow in a spike or raceme, often with a similarly colored bract below each flower. Most botanists now include the Wintergreen Family in the Heath Family.

There are five, rarely four, petals and sepals. The petals may be separate (prince's pine, wintergreen), partly united (azalea), or completely united into vase-shaped flowers (heather and pine drops). The lower petal in some may be somewhat larger and more highly colored. Flowers may be red, pinkish or white with five to ten stamens. The calyx is persistent. The ovary, usually five-celled and superior, has a long persistent style. The fruit may be a berry (blueberry, cranberry), but most Heaths produce a hard capsule. This capsule, split into five parts, often persists, standing or hanging from its stem through the winter months. Many are useful for dried arrangements. Found, usually in mountainous areas, over much of North America, Europe, and Asia.

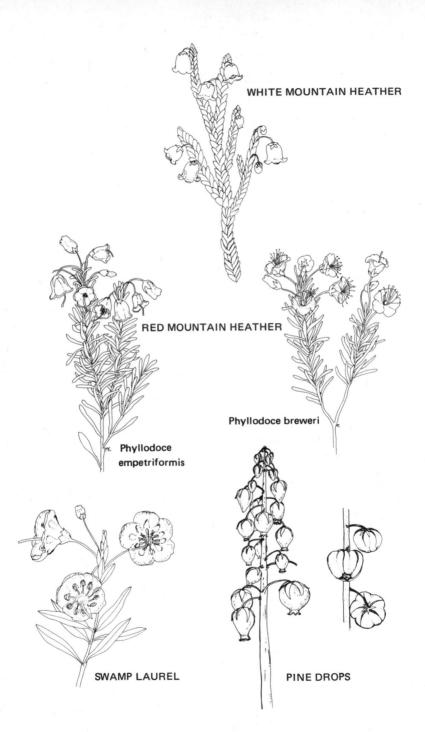

WHITE MOUNTAIN HEATHER

RED MOUNTAIN HEATHER

Phyllodoce breweri

Phyllodoce
empetriformis

SWAMP LAUREL

PINE DROPS

White Mountain Heather, *Cassiope mertensiana,* is a lovely white heather found from the high Sierra Nevada north to Alaska. It grows in granite nooks and ledges, especially along streams or rocky lake edges at 8,000-10,000 feet. This tiny alpine plant, only 2-12 inches (5-30 cm) high, has small hanging white flowers resembling lily-of-the-valley. Each bell-shaped flower swings from a bright red pedicel; the calyx is also red. The evergreen scale-like leaves completely cover the stem in a four-angled pattern. This is a great favorite of high mountain hikers.

Red Heather, *Phyllodoce empetriformis, Phyllodoce breweri,* are two red heathers of the mountainous West. *Phyllodoce empetriformis* grows further north and has hanging bell-like flowers very similar to those of the white heather. *Phyllodoce breweri* has larger flowers, ½ inch (1.3 cm) across, which are more upright and saucer-shaped. The calyx and pedicel may be reddish also. The filaments are so long they stand above the corolla. Both species have narrow, linear leaves which stand out stiffly all along the low branches. Red heather grows 8-10 inches (20-25 cm) high, in mountains of the Northwest and the Rockies, up to 12,000 feet.

Swamp Laurel, Bog Laurel, *Kalmia polifolio,* is a plant that grows best in cool places. It is found along streams and wet areas over much of North America. It often is an alpine flower near timberline (parts of Rockies, Sierra, Cascades), but will be found at lower elevations in cool spots. It really is a miniature shrub.

The five-lobed, rose-colored corolla opens wide into a shallow saucer. There are ten tiny depressions or pouches in this saucer, each holding a stamen. As the petals expand, the filaments bend upward, but the anthers are held tightly in their depressions. As pollen shedding time approaches, an insect lighting on the corolla will disturb the filaments, the anthers will snap out, shaking off their pollen. One of the red mountain heathers, *Phyllodoce breweri,* resembles this plant, but the heather neither opens as flat (is more urn-shaped) nor does it have the stamen pouches. Two to ten flowers are clustered, each on a slender reddish stem. The leaves are leathery, evergreen ½-1 inch (1.3-2.5 cm) and are whitish underneath. The calyx persists around the five-valve capsule. All parts except the wood are poisonous to sheep, cattle, and humans.

Pine Drops, *Pterospora andromeda,* grow on tall, unbranched, brown or purplish stalks, often many in a cluster, 12-48 inches (30-120 cm) high. The flowers are in a long raceme, usually whitish or reddish, and are hanging, closed bell-shaped flowers. The sepals are colored like the stems; they dry a rich brown and persist on the stiff hairy stalks through winter snow. The narrow brown modified leaves are found along the lower part of the stem. They bloom from June to August, usually in open pine forests where there is much decaying plant material. They are widely distributed across North America from Canada south through the regions of the Atlantic Coast, Great Lakes, Rockies, Sierra, and south into Mexico.

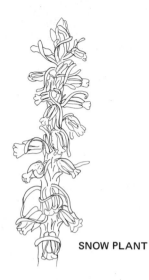

SNOW PLANT

BLUE GENTIAN

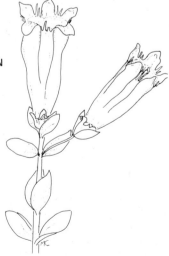

Snow Plant, *Sarcodes sanguinea,* is a bright-red plant growing where there is thick humus in coniferous woods at elevations of 4,000-8,000 feet, often while there are still many snowbanks. It is a dramatic plant, appearing early in the spring, suddenly, and with no green parts! The thick, fleshy, scaly stem and the many closely packed hanging flowers are all crimson color. There may be one stem at a place, or many stems, 6-20 inches (15-50 cm) tall. The leaves are large crimson strap-like scales, more numerous on the lower portion of the stalk. The flowers are bright crimson, ½-1 inch (1.3-2.5 cm) long, bell-shaped, with the corolla showing five deep lobes. The sepals are separate and are almost as big as the corolla lobes and as brilliantly colored. There are ten red stamens. The petals and sepals are persistent around the five-part red ovary.

Once seen, snow plant will never be forgotten or mistaken. It blooms in May to July in the Sierra, Coast Range of California, southern Oregon, western Nevada, and northern Lower California.

GENTIAN FAMILY
Gentianaceae

Gentian is a widespread family in temperate regions all over the world, with the most beautiful ones in the high mountains. Western Gentians are mountain species, so are not as well known as those in the eastern or central United States or Canada. They usually are small herbs, though the green gentian grows up to 6 feet (2m) tall. They have an odorless but bitter juice. The opposite leaves are smooth-margined and sessile. The sepals are fused except at the tip, and are five-toothed (sometimes four). The petals are united into a corolla tube, with the lobes free, and are of the same number as calyx lobes. Corolla lobes overlap or twist in the bud. The stamens alternate with the petal lobes and are attached to the throat of the corolla. The superior ovary has two stigmas, the seeds forming in a two-sided capsule; the corolla remaining and drying. The flowers may be deep blue, yellow, rose-pink or green-white. Found in the high Rockies, Sierra, Alps, Himalayas, and Andes. At lower elevations species can be found in damp meadows where the climate is temperate. Some species have medicinal value. The fringed gentian is a common garden plant of the East.

Blue Gentian, Mountain Gentian, *Gentiana calycosa,* is one of the most beautiful high mountain flowers. It is a darker blue than the fringed gentian. The erect bell shaped flower usually has just one bloom for each 2-8 inch (5-20 cm) stem; if others, they come from the upper leaf axils. It is a perennial from a rootcrown, forming a thick mat with shiny heavy ½-1 inch (1.3-5.2 cm) long leaves. Several blooming stems grow from one clump, and at the height of the season, each clump is a mass of color.

SHOOTING STARS

The calyx is small, quite brown and membranous. The five corolla lobes and the inside of the bell are deep blue; the outside of the bell may be paler, showing definite dark veins. Between each two rounded corolla lobes there is a yellow dotted area. The corolla tube is about 1½ inches (4 cm) long. It blooms in the late summer and into fall, July to September, opening in the mornings and closing in the afternoons. Grows from 7,000-10,000 feet, British Columbia to Montana, south in the Rocky Mountains and westward into the Sierra Nevada.

PRIMROSE FAMILY
Primulaceae

All Primroses are plants with five petals, at least partly united, and with simple, undivided leaves. The stamens are opposite the petals, not alternate as with most plants. There is a single style and stigma. The flowers are perfect, regular, symmetrical, on the plan of five, with a superior ovary. The fruit is a capsule. The lovely primroses and cyclamens which grow in shady gardens are favorites in this family.

Shooting Star, Mosquito Bills, Sailor Caps, *Dodecatheon pauciflorum*   The blossoms of shooting star seem turned inside out, for the corolla and calyx are deeply cut and turn back away from the stamens and pistil. Several magenta, lavender-pink, or sometimes white flowers grow in an umbel on the top of a slender stem. Usually there are bands of white, yellow, or purple at the base of the petals. The stamens, with thick filaments, closely surround the single pistil and style. These parts often look like a beak or bill which gives one of the common names. They point downwards toward the thick round basal leaves. As the petals fade and drop, the calyx turns up and protects the capsule. There are many species in the West; in the mountains they grow mainly in damp meadows. *Dodecatheon pauciflorum* is a common species, found from low valleys to high mountains. The petals are bright rose purple, ½-1 inch (1.3-2.5 cm) long, growing on 6-16 inch (15-40 cm) stalks. *Dodecatheon jeffreyi* is a taller, stouter plant, usually found from 4,000 feet upward. *Dodecatheon hendersonii* is a common California species, growing 9-14 inches (22.5-35 cm) tall on moist hillsides, often with Johnny-jump-ups and buttercups, blooming from February through March. The California Indians roasted the roots and leaves of this species.

Lowland Shooting Star, *Dodecatheon patulum,* is pale and small with purple filaments.

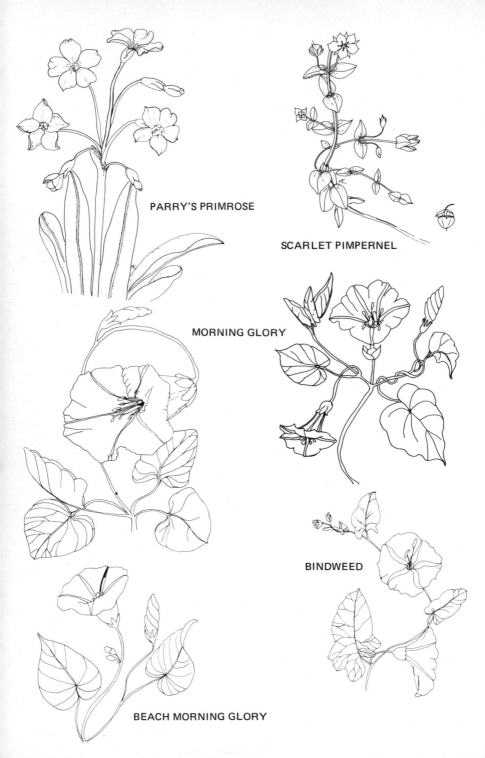

PARRY'S PRIMROSE

SCARLET PIMPERNEL

MORNING GLORY

BINDWEED

BEACH MORNING GLORY

Parry's Primrose, *Primula parryi,* is a distinctive blood-red to rose-red flower found in the high mountains of the West, growing and blooming along streams or in rock ledges soon after the snow melts. The plant has a strong odor and large succulent smooth leaves, 4-12 inches (10-30 cm) long, in a basal clump. There are many flowers in an umbel, each flower ½-¾ inch (1.3-1.8 cm) across.

Scarlet Pimpernel, Poor Man's Weatherglass, *Anagallis arvensis,* really is more of a coral color than scarlet. It opens only in sunny weather. It is a small flower about ⅓ inch (.8 cm) across, growing on weak stems which may be 1 foot (30 cm) long. The small opposite leaves are entire and sessile. The five rounded petals are joined just at the base, often with a darker color band. The calyx is deeply divided into five narrow lobes. The fruit is a round capsule which opens with a lid. Though a lovely flower, it is considered a weed all over America and Europe. It grows everywhere, but prefers mild climates where it blooms most of the year if it gets enough water. A blue variety is often found.

MORNING GLORY FAMILY
Convolvulaceae

This family was given its name because *Convolvulus* means "to twine." This flower is well-known, with the corolla often very showy, opening in the morning hours. The five-lobed corolla is twisted in the bud. The five sepals are separate and stay on to protect the capsule. The pistil is two-celled, each cell producing two seeds. The parasitic plant, dodder, belongs to this family, as can be seen from the flower structure. It produces no green parts and depends on the plants it twines around for its food. It looks like yellow-orange string winding and trailing over, under, and through other plants.

Morning Glory, *Convolvulus subacaulis.*   This small, trailing plant growing amid filaree, poppies, and other wildflowers does not produce long runners. The flower is white or cream-colored, with purplish streaks on the outside. The leaves are almost heart-shaped, thin and slightly hairy. The calyx is partly enclosed by two bracts. The stamens are attached to the corolla, the style divided near the tip. The round capsule holds four seeds.

Bindweed, *Convolvulus arvensis*   This whitish Morning Glory is a native of Europe and has become one of our worst weeds. Long stems grow from long, strong, deep perennial roots, all of which tangle farm machinery. It spreads very rapidly and is extremely hard to get rid of. The flower is much like that of the native species, except that the corolla edge is smooth. Blooms in fields and orchards in March to May.

Convolvulus soldanella is a species found along the whole Pacific Coast. The stems grow 1-1½ feet (30-45 cm) long with thick, deep green, shiny leaves. The funnel-shaped corolla is pinkish or pale lavender.

BIRD'S EYE GILIA

GLOBE GILIA

SCARLET GILIA

ALPINE PHLOX

GILIA or PHLOX FAMILY
Polemoniaceae

Mostly a family of low-growing herbs, though some develop woody bases; most of them have small flowers. Leaves vary in size and shape; the five-part calyx persists, and five-lobe or five-point corolla is twisted in the bud. Stamens are attached to the corolla tube, and alternate with the lobes. The superior ovary develops into a three-celled capsule with many seeds.

Bird's Eye Gilia, *Gilia tricolor,* is a common spring wildflower of California and very distinctive with its three-color corolla. The lobes are light blue, throat top is dark blue with spots, the rest is yellow. The blossoms are clustered atop slender stems. The leaves are finely cut. It grows in open foothill country, 100–3,000 feet elevation, in the Coast Ranges, Central Valley, and Sierran hills of California.

Globe Gilia, *Gilia capitata*   You notice this flower because the small blossoms are closely crowded into dense round clusters or heads at the top of slender leafless stalks, making spots of clear blue, white, or lavender color. A common flower of open slopes and sandy areas, 200-5,000 feet in California, north to Washington. The stamens stand taller than the corolla, so the head looks like a pincushion. The calyx is hairy, the leaves mostly basal.

Scarlet Gilia, Firecracker, Skyrocket, *Gilia (Ipomopsis) aggregata*   The common names of this flower are descriptive—these are brilliant red flowers having a funnel-shaped corolla with pointed lobes which turn or curve back. The flowers crowd near the stalk ends forming a mass of color. Much color variation can be found in the flowers, with scarlet shading through pinks to white. The slender plants have several blooming stalks growing from a perennial basal rosette of finely divided leaves. They grow on sunny slopes, moist roadsides, sandy areas all over the West, 4,000-10,000 feet elevation.

Alpine Phlox, *Phlox douglasii,* is a low, spreading plant with woody stems, the plant covered with many narrow pointed leaves. During the summer it is a mass of little white, pink, or purple flowers about ¾ inch (1,8 cm) across. The five petals are united into a tube about 1 inch (2.5 cm) long. The calyx is shorter than the tube and is divided into five pointed, hairy parts. This phlox grows in high mountains 4,700-10,300 feet all over America, from the Atlantic to Pacific, Mexico to Canada. Phlox have been developed for gardens, and there are also many tall species.

Western Polemonium, Jacob's Ladder, *Polemonium occidentale (caeruleum),* is a slender, single-stemmed plant 1½-3 feet (45-90 cm) tall with the upper leaves much smaller. The leaves are compound, with seven

WESTERN JACOB'S LADDER

SKY PILOT

to fifteen pairs of leaflets, with the top three usually joined. The arrangement of these leaflets up the petiole probably gives many of the species the
common name of Jacob's ladder. The flowers are purplish-blue, shaped
like a wide-open bell, paler inside and veined with blue. The style extends
far beyond the corolla. Jacob's ladder likes wet areas 2,000-10,000 feet,
British Columbia to southern California, east to Colorado.

Sky Pilot, Skunk Polemonium, *Polemonium viscosum*   This funnel-
shaped blue or lavender species with orange anthers looks more beautiful
than its odor. When its leaves are crushed, the odor is very skunk-like. It
grows from 7,000-12,000 feet all through the Rockies, to Arizona, and
west to Washington. The leaves are slightly sticky and mostly basal. As in
all Polemoniums, they are compound, but the thirty to forty leaflets are
also three- to five-lobed and are small, so they appear whorled around the
stem, not "ladder-like." It enjoys moist places, growing even in high
sunny meadows if they are damp enough, especially liking moist rock
crevices.

Jacob's Ladder, *Polemonium albiflorum*   This common white-flowered
species of woods and moist areas of the Rocky Mountains, often makes
whole areas a froth of whiteness. Several stems grow from the base, with
many flower clusters atop each. The leaves are divided into small side
leaflets, evenly spaced (typical Jacob's ladder). The petals have a dark
line down the center, and the big yellow anthers stand higher than the
corolla. The upper stems and sepals are quite hairy.

Polemonium reptans is a creeping species with pale blue flowers which
grows in the East. There are several species of Jacob's ladder which are
common wildflowers of the European Alps.

PHACELIA or WATERLEAF FAMILY
Hydrophyllaceae

Different members of the Phacelia Family may bloom singly on a
stem, in heads, or in coiled spikes like the neck of a fiddle. The
individual blossoms, however, are very similar. The five petals are
united at the base, with the corolla appearing like a cup or saucer.
The five long stamens are attached near the base of the corolla,
alternate with the lobes, and extend well beyond the corolla. The
pistil is two-celled; in some there is just one style that is divided at
the tip while in others there are two distinct styles. The ovary is
superior. The leaves are of many shapes, opposite or alternate. The
plants usually are quite hairy. This family is a favorite of bees.

BABY BLUE EYES

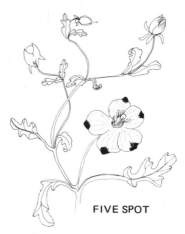

FIVE SPOT

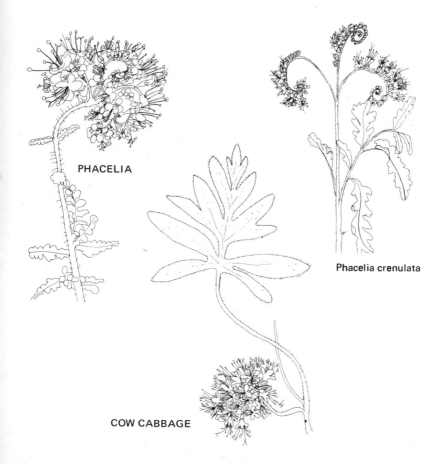

PHACELIA

Phacelia crenulata

COW CABBAGE

Baby Blue Eyes, Nemophila menziesii   This lovely cup-shaped, sky-blue or deep blue wildflower is often found in moist spots in the valleys or on protected hillsides. The corolla is lighter near the center and often is veined or spotted. The flowers grow on slender stems from the leaf axils, the plants growing from 3-18 inches (7.5-45 cm) tall. Ten nectar glands are arranged at the base of the stamens. There is a projection, like a spur, between each two of the five deeply cut calyx lobes. The leaves are divided into many small lobes, and are opposite. This lovely flower is also grown in gardens. Blooms from February to April, depending on altitude, from 50-5,000 feet in coastal and Sierran California.

Five Spot, Calico Flower, *Nemophila maculata,* is a striking flower with five white petal-lobes and rows of purple dots radiating from the center to a large purple spot at the end of each lobe. Flowers grow singly on each of the several 5-10 inch (12.5-25 cm) stems. The leaves are broadly oblong, with two or three lobes. Blossoms from April to August, depending on elevation, in California Sierran and coastal hills and valleys.

Phacelia, Waterleaf, *Phacelia ciliata*   There are a great many Phacelias in the West. The petals are blue, purple, or white, falling early; the calyx becomes papery and surrounds the two-cell capsule. The flowers are in coiled heads that unwind as the buds open. *Phacelia ciliata* has blue petals, deeply cut sepals, and long stamens with nectar glands near their base. The stems, 9-14 inches (22.5-35 cm) long branch from the base. The leaves are deeply divided, alternately arranged. This species grows in valleys and hillsides up to 5,000 feet over most of California and into Lower California, often growing in great masses. Flowers in March and April.

Phacelia crenulata is a desert species, found in New Mexico, Arizona and southern California, and into Lower California. Its lovely violet-purple flowers bloom along uncurling hairy flower stalks. Leaves usually have five hairy leaflets, with the tip leaflet much bigger; the calyx is also very sticky and hairy. The anthers are whitish with purple filaments. Often forms large clumps in dry areas, making a splash of color.

Cow Cabbage, Squaw Cabbage, Cat's Breeches, *Hydrophyllum capitatum,* is a low-growing plant with leaves much taller than the round head of white to pale lavender-blue flowers. The long stamens are the noticeable part of the flower. The leaves are broad, succulent, pinnately divided, and so shaped that they will hold water when it rains. The plant has a long fleshy root. The Indians used both the roots and the leaves for food. Found in pine woods and moist ravines from Canada south to Oregon, Utah and Colorado. Blooms in May and June.

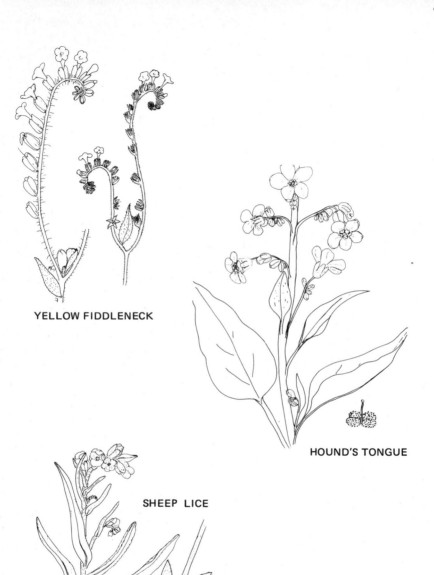

YELLOW FIDDLENECK

HOUND'S TONGUE

SHEEP LICE

BORAGE FAMILY
Boraginaceae

Members of the Borage Family have rather small flowers growing along one-sided coiled spikes, resembling the neck of a fiddle, and similar to some members of the Phacelia Family. They unroll as the buds open. The family is very like the Phacelia Family, with hairy stems and leaves, but the ovary develops into nutlets which break apart when ripe, and is the primary characteristic of this family. The leaves are simple, alternate, 1-9 inches (2.5-22.5 cm) long. Blue forget-me-not and the fragrant heliotrope are garden Borages, and most of the wild members of the family resemble them. Forget-me-not is the state flower of Alaska.

Yellow Fiddleneck, Buckthorn Weed, *Amsinckia douglasiana, Amsinckia spectabilis, Amsinckia intermedia*   This well-known wildflower with many local names has small, yellow to deep orange, vase-shaped flowers, with five flaring lobes. They are strung along one side of a tightly coiled stem, 1-4 feet (30-120 cm) high. The stems, leaves, and calyx are covered with short, stiff, prickly hairs. *Amsinckia douglasiana,* with long, often rusty hairs, is the common yellow fiddleneck of the interior valleys of California. *Amsinckia intermedia* is a small yellowish fiddleneck common in grassy open places below 5,000 feet, from the Sierra Nevada to the Coast Ranges, south to Lower California and Arizona, and north to Oregon, Washington, and Idaho. *Amsinckia spectabilis* is quite orange, with larger flowers and the plant usually more branched. It grows along coastal areas from Lower California into Oregon.

Fiddlenecks are found in almost any valley, field, or hillside from March to June. Since the nutlets make good food for animals, the plant is sometimes called saccato gordo meaning "fat grass."

Hound's Tongue, *Cynoglossum grande*   The leaves of this flower have given it its common name because of their shape. They are 3-8 inches (7.5-20 cm) long, mostly basal. The 1-4 foot (30-120 cm) erect stems are not hairy. Both the color and the shape of the flowers are unusually lovely. The five blue united petals are a little longer than they are wide and the throat of the tube shades to pink-lavender and is ringed with little white bumps; the buds may be pink also. The calyx tube ends in narrow, oblong, hairy lobes. The fruit is composed of four large nutlets, covered with barbed prickles, forming a bur. Hound's tongue can be found in wooded canyons 100-4,000 feet in the Coast Ranges and Sierra Nevada of California, north to Washington. It is one of the early spring flowers.

Sheep Lice, *Cynoglossum officínale* is a magenta-colored close relative that grows all over America from Quebec to the Pacific and south to Arkansas. The flowers seem to stay cup-shaped, not opening flat. The nutlets open out flat, but stay attached to the base of the style; surfaces are covered with barbed hairs. The flowering coil keeps growing as seeds mature so the persistent nutlets are scattered on a long spray.

POPCORN FLOWER

LUNGWORT

Popcorn Flower, *Plagiobothrys nothofulvus,* is a slender hairy annual with tiny white blossoms which cluster closely together, giving the appearance of a popped kernel of corn; leaves mostly basal. The corolla, ¼ - ⅓ inch (.6-.8 cm) across, is short, with a ring of crests at the mouth of the throat. The upper part of the rusty-haired calyx falls off as the cluster of one to four, usually three, nutlets ripen, the lower part persisting as a shallow cup to hold them. The stem may be purplish at the base. Found from Mexico to Canada in foothills and valleys of the West, 100-3,000 feet elevation, blooming March to May. There are many close relatives, all looking like tiny white forget-me-nots.

Lungwort, Mountain Bluebell, Mertensia, *Mertensia ciliata,* grow in the moist areas of western mountains from 5,000 to 10,000 feet; other closely related species grow in the East from New York to South Carolina, spreading west as far as Ontario and Kansas. All species are very lovely wildflowers, with drooping blue racemes on plants 2-5 feet (60-150 cm) tall. The flowers are trumpet-shaped with tubes about ½ inch (1.3 cm) long, with the broad filaments of the stamens growing alternately on the tubes. The flowers of several species are rosy-pink in the bud (or when withering), but blue when open. *Mertensia ciliata* is light blue, with small yellow-tipped crests at the top of the tube. The leaves of this Borage are smooth, not rough as are most members in the family. The upper leaves are sessile. The plants grow from perennial roots as soon as the earth begins warming, so by following spring up the mountain, you can find lungwort in bloom most of the long summer.

BLUEBELL or BELLFLOWER FAMILY
Campanulaceae

The lovely hanging, blue, bell-like flowers are the characteristic features of this family. The perennial plants are small, with several slender stems. The basal leaves are simple, round or oval, usually producing a milky juice. They may dry and wither early. The bell-shaped corolla is five-lobed with flaring tips. The two- to five-celled ovary is inferior, with the calyx tube fused to it except at the tips. The five stamens are attached to the corolla at the point where the calyx tips are free. The one long style has two to five stigmas, which open long after the flower first opens. The fruit is a many-seeded capsule. This is a large, widely distributed family all over the world, from low elevation to high mountains. Many species have been developed into beautiful garden plants.

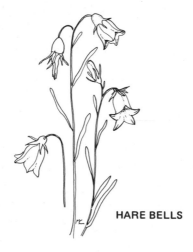

HARE BELLS

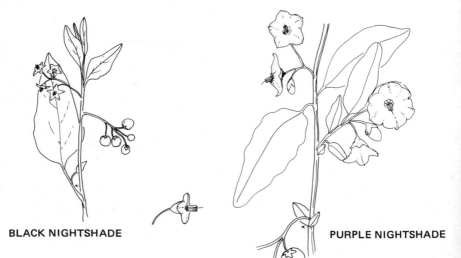

BLACK NIGHTSHADE

PURPLE NIGHTSHADE

Hare Bells, Blue Bells of Scotland, *Campanula rotundifolia,* a dainty hanging bell-like flower found all across our continent and throughout Europe and Asia. There are many slender flowering stalks, 6-20 inches (1450 cm) high with one to nine blossoms each. The buds are erect, but as they open, they hang downwards. The anthers are pale yellow or sometimes bluish. The fused part of the calyx is closely attached to the inferior ovary, persisting and drying to the capsule.

Bluebells are common mountain flowers, usually from 5,000-12,000 feet elevation, blooming from July to September. They grow also in lower elevations, and are found in dry to moist slopes and fields, even among sagebrush. Plants show much variation in height, leaf, and hairiness of leaves, but always with the lovely hanging blue bells.

NIGHTSHADE or POTATO FAMILY
Solanaceae

Nightshades grow all over the world, but are especially abundant in the tropics. Some of our best known foods belong to this family, including potatoes, tomatoes, eggplant and bell peppers, chilies and cayenne peppers; however, some wild species of this family have poisonous berries, especially when unripe. Petunias are familiar garden flower members; also included are tobacco, ground cherry, and bittersweet. All have a five-lobed corolla, folded in the bud; some are funnel-shaped, but most are saucer-like. The five, almost sessile, stamens are inserted in the corolla, alternately with its lobes. The two-celled superior ovary has one style and a one- or two-lobed stigma. The fruit is a berry or capsule.

Black Nightshade, *Solanum nigrum,* may be white, yellow or purple. The plants have many branches, with the flowers in loose umbels blooming over a long season, so there will be buds, flowers, and berries all at the same time. A common one in fields and open places over most of the United States and southern Canada is the black nightshade, *Solanum nigrum.* It was introduced from Europe and has small white star-like flowers ¼ inch (.5-.6 cm) across and black berries. Purple nightshade or blue witch, *Solanum umbelliferum,* has a shallow, almost tubeless corolla from ½-¾ inch (1.3-1.8 cm) wide, ruffled between the lobes, with five pairs of green glands near the base of the lobes. The bright yellow anthers stand together at the center with almost no filaments, forming a cylinder around the style. The purple to white flowers grow in loose umbels of buds, flowers and bright green berries which turn whitish with a green base. The stems may be woody at the base, branching or even becoming vine-like. Found in cool gulches of California and Nevada, mainly May and June, but continuing to bloom a good part of the year. Berries are said to be poisonous.

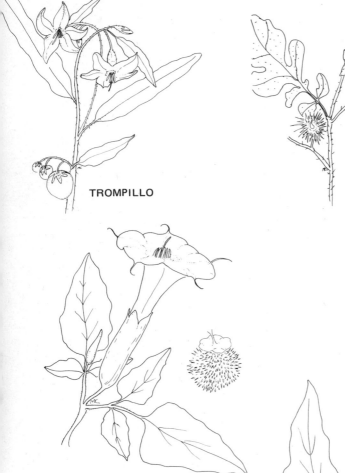
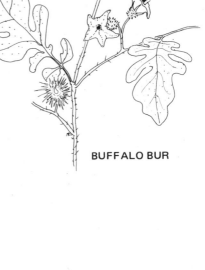

TROMPILLO

BUFFALO BUR

THORN APPLE

JIMSON WEED

142

Trompillo, Desert Nightshade, *Solanum elaeagnifolium,* is the common nightshade in Texas, and has come into the Far West from the Great Plains. The leafy stems vary from being very prickly to completely spineless. Flowers are violet or blue, berries a dull yellow. The lowest stamen is much larger than the other four. A yellow-flowered, yellow-spined Nightshade called buffalo bur, *Solanum rostratum,* has also come in from the Great Plains. Its sepals, surrounding the developing berry, are very prickly.

Thorn Apple, Tolguacha, *Datura wrightii (inoxia) (meteloides),* is a large white-flowered plant, spreading but erect, which covers large areas. The trumpet-shaped flowers, shaded with lavender, are 3-6 inches (7.5-15 cm) across and stand above the big gray-green leaves. They open in late afternoon and close soon after sunrise next day. Each corolla lobe has a long slender thread-like projection at the tip. The calyx, tipped with five short teeth, encloses most of the throat of the trumpet, the lower part persisting as a collar. The capsule is round and covered with prickles. Grows mostly along sandy roadsides, field, and gully areas in valley and desert areas of central and southern California to Mexico and South America, east to southern Utah and Texas.

Jimson Weed, *Datura stramonium,* is not as common as the thorn apple, but is more widely distributed for it is found in waste places over much of the U.S. It has fewer branches, is an annual, and the white flowers are only 1½-3 inches (3.8-7.5) across. It is a native of tropical America, but now grows and blooms all summer in the West and over many parts of the U.S. It contains many poisonous alkaloids.

FIGWORT FAMILY
Scrophulariaceae

Most members of the Figwort Family have five united petals not all alike, so are included in the next chapter. However, mullein, *Verbascum thapsus,* has five corolla lobes which are very similar, the two upper ones only slightly smaller. All five petals are so much alike that this flower fits better in this chapter. This tall, stiff, unbranched, semi-woody plant was introduced from Europe, but now grows practically all over North America along roadsides and on dry slopes up to 8,000 feet. The plant appears velvety because of thick white hairs.

This biennial forms an attractive large thick basal rosette with leaves 4-10 inches (10-25 cm) long. The next spring, a tall flower stalk grows, with progressively smaller leaves tightly attached by half the length of the midvein along the stem. The flower head is a closely crowded 5-15 inch spike, with open bright yellow flowers irregularly scattered among buds and maturing capsules.

There are five stamens with anthers (the only group in Figworts where this is true), the three upper ones wooly beneath the anther. The stigma is small and the style tips it forward so it lies along the face of the lowest petal. The calyx grows after the corolla falls, protecting the capsule. The stalk is very woody and often stands through several seasons. The fruits on it are the source of winter food for birds, since it sticks up through snow and matted debris.

MULLEIN

HEDGE NETTLE

Chapter IX

FIVE UNITED PETALS
NOT ALL ALIKE

Many flowers with five united petals which are not all alike might be considered "queer-shaped." Most of them have a tubular corolla that is "two-lipped," each lip having two or three lobes. Many of them are very beautiful; snapdragons are common garden examples. The Mint Family and the Figwort Family are included in this group.

MINT FAMILY
Labitae

The Mint Family is very large. The leaves have a strong mint odor when crushed and grow opposite each other in pairs up the square stem. The opposite leaves and square stem are excellent clues to identify Mints. The corolla is two-lipped, usually with two lobes in the upper lip and three in the lower, the flowers growing in whorls. The calyx usually is five-toothed and may be two-lipped. There usually are four stamens, standing in pairs on the corolla tube. The ovary is superior, with four lobes, separating into four smooth little nutlets. Many members of this family are herbs used for cooking, like sage and thyme. Hoarhound, wood mint, and skullcap are eastern and midwestern examples of the family. Stinging nettles are unpleasant members.

Hedge Nettle, *Stachys bullata,* is a common member of the Mint Family that grows along the roads as a coarse weed 10-22 inches (25-55 cm) high with rough and hairy leaves and stems; however, it is not a stinging nettle. The flowers may be bright pink to purple or pale lavender about 1/3 inch (.8 cm) long, streaked and speckled with darker shades. About six flowers per whorl grow near the top of the square stem, the whorls are ½-1 inch (1.3-2.5 cm) apart. Grows in Washington, Oregon, and California.

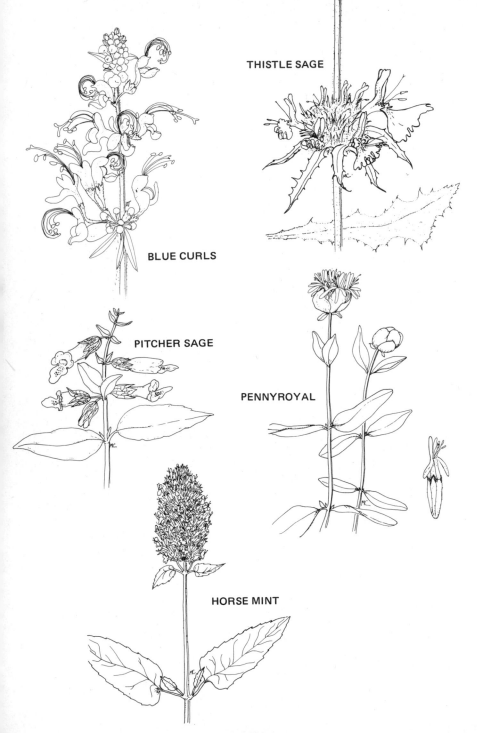

THISTLE SAGE

BLUE CURLS

PITCHER SAGE

PENNYROYAL

HORSE MINT

146

Bluecurls, *Trichostema lanceolatum,* is a most unusual looking flower. The bright blue corolla is nearly an inch (2.5 cm) long, covered with fuzzy, pink wool, giving it a changeable effect which seems irridescent. The purple stamens and style are twice as long as the corolla, and very conspicuous. The plant is shrubby, with many stems, growing 2-4 feet (60-120 cm) high, on rocky hills in southern California. It was used for medicine by the early Spanish-Californians. Sometimes it is called camphor weed, because of the strong, unpleasant odor. It blooms from late spring to fall, and is an important bee plant. It is pollinated by the day-flying sphinx moths.

Thistle Sage, *Salvia carduacea,* is an extremely beautiful flower with a stout purple stem all covered with white wool, and bright blue-lilac flowers almost covered by woolly bracts and the woolly two-lipped calyx. The large pale, spine-tipped basal rosette of leaves are also thickly covered with white wool. The corolla is two-lipped, with the middle lobe of the lower lip fan-shaped and fringed. The pistil is purple and the anthers are bright orange. The flowers grow in tiers around the square stem. The leaves have a strong sage odor. Thistle sage grows in central and southern California on low foothill slopes and dry open plains, blooming in the spring and summer.

Pitcher Sage, *Lepechinia (Sphacele) calycina,* is a shrubby plant with flowers somewhat resembling white or pale pink monkey flower, growing in central and southern California, blooming in spring and summer. The corolla tube has four lobes much alike, and one longer lobe. The leaves smell like sage, but the flowers do not look much like sage blossoms.

Horse Mint, Giant Hyssop, *Agastache urticifolia,* is a tall mint, 2-5 feet (60-150 cm) with many stems from the base, each with many opposite branches. The tiny white to lavender flowers are crowded into dense spikes atop each branch. The spike color mainly comes from the five purplish calyx teeth surrounding each lighter-colored flower. The stamens are much longer than the corolla, especially one of the pairs. The leaves resemble nettle, but have no stinging hairs. Grows in moist spots from foothills to 8,000 feet from Montana to British Columbia, south to Colorado and California. Often abundant in open meadows and aspen areas.

Pennyroyal, *Monardella odoratissima*   The scientific name for this light lavender flower describes one of its most distinguishing characteristics- —the leaves are very aromatic when crushed, and the plant can be recognized by its odor even before it is in bloom. It is a sharp odor, perhaps described as a cross between mint and sage, easily remembered once smelled. Pennyroyal is a perennial, forming a woody-based clump. Many small typical-mint flowers are tightly grouped into a head surrounded by bracts, one head at the top of each 8-12 inch (20-30 cm) stem. The bracts are usually reddish-purple, much deeper color than the fragile-appearing individual flowers.

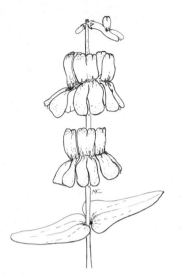

CHINESE HOUSES

COMMON MONKEY FLOWER

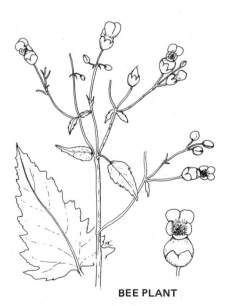

BEE PLANT

FIGWORT FAMILY
Scrophulariaceae

Snapdragon, monkey flower, paintbrush, and penstemon are all members of this very colorful family. The five united petals form an irregular corolla, usually two-lipped and modified for insect attraction. Often the flowers have dots or lead lines for the bees, and most of them produce lots of nectar. The lower lip is a "landing platform" for insects. The calyx is five-lobed, sometimes irregular. The flowers are complete, usually with four stamens. A fifth stamen is present in penstemons, hence the name, but it has no anther. Mullein is the only Figwort that has five stamens all with anthers (see page 143). The stamens are attached to the throat of the corolla in pairs. The superior ovary is two-celled, never four-divided on the outside, and forms a many-seeded capsule.

Chinese Houses, *Collinsia heterophylla (bicolor)*   The strange name of this flower comes from the tiers of blossoms growing in whorls, often closely spaced, on the slender branching 6-18 inch (15-45 cm) stems. The tiers look something like the flaring roof lines of Chinese houses. The corolla has a short tube, the throat opening into two lips. The white upper lip has two erect lobes; the pinkish-lavender or white lower lip is large, three-lobed, with the middle lobe keel-shaped, enclosing the four stamens and the style. There is a gland at the base of the corolla. The leaves are broadly oblong and pointed, almost sessile. This flower is common in the foothills all over coastal California, from the sea to 2,800 feet.

Bee Plant, *Scrophularia californica,* is a tall-growing perennial plant, 3-6 feet (1-2 cm) high, with opposite leaves. It grows in moist spots over most of California, north to British Columbia. The flowers are small, ½ inch (1.3 cm), dark red, with the upper lip larger, and all lobes upright except the short middle lower one. The throat is plump and dark, making the flower look like a tiny face. A many-seeded capsule develops. It blooms from March to June. There are many varieties; a closely related species grows in the Rockies. Each flower has a nectar cup, and you can find this flower at times by looking where the bee hum is loudest.

Common Monkey Flower, *Mimulus guttatus*   There are many, many species of monkey flower. This is the most common, found in the West where there are low moist fields and streambanks. The plant has a hollow stem and grows 1-2 feet (30-60 cm) high, either as an annual or as a perennial. There are several branches with many large brilliant yellow flowers on pedicels from leaf axils. The lower lip is broad and two ridges run into the purple or brown-dotted throat. The pistil has a two-lipped stigma that will close when touched. The corolla falls early, and the five-angled, five-toothed big calyx protects the thick-walled capsule. The opposite leaves are thin, smooth, and unevenly toothed. The lower leaves have stems, the upper ones are sessile. Blooms in April, on into summer.

DESERT MONKEY FLOWER

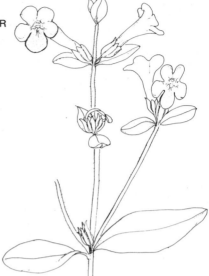

STICKY MONKEY FLOWER

PINK MONKEY FLOWER

Flower with bract

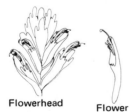

Flowerhead   Flower

FLOWER DETAIL OF CASTILLEJA

Desert Monkey Flower, *Mimulus bigelovi,* is a small creeping plant which rarely grows more than 8 inches (20 cm) tall. The flowers are large, ½-1 inch (1.3-2.5 cm), several to each branch. The corolla is crimson with a yellow, purple-dotted throat. This *Mimulus* grows on dry desert mountain slopes or flats from 500-6,000 feet in California, Arizona, Colorado, Utah, and Texas.

Sticky Monkey Flower, *Mimulus (Diplacus) longiflorus,* is an evergreen bush 2-4 feet (60-120 cm), which has deep green opposite leaves. The leaves and stems are sticky. The tubular flowers are two-lipped on short pedicels, arranged in whorls. They usually are orange-yellow, but may be deep orange to pale cream color, with two deep orange ridges in the throat. The calyx is five-toothed and angular. The two-lobed stigma will close if touched. Grows on dry slopes below 5,000 feet in central and southern California.

Bush Monkey Flower, *Mimulus (Diplacus) aurantiacus,* is a northern species with orange or orange-yellow blooms growing on the rocky hills and canyon sides below 3,000 feet of Sierra and Coast Ranges and western Oregon, blooming from April to September. It has a very sticky calyx and long, ½-1 inch (1.3-2.5 cm), pedicel.

Pink Monkey Flower, *Mimulus lewisii,* is a striking pink flower of the high mountains, found along streams and moist rock ledges. The plant grows 6-24 inches (15-60 cm) high, often in thick clumps. The flowers vary in color from light to deep, deep pink. The characteristic two-lipped corolla is protected by the sharp-tipped and quite angled calyx. Two high yellow ridges run from the lower lip of the corolla down into the throat. The flowers are pedicellate, often blooming in pairs, one from each with the longer pair attached to the front of the throat at the base of the yellow ridges; both pairs bend to fit tightly against the upper throat. The corolla falls early, but the calyx persists to enclose the capsule with many tiny seeds. Found in the high mountains of the West, 8,000-10,000 feet, blooming in July and August.

Paintbrush, Painted Cup, Castilleja, are common, beautiful wildflowers, looking like brushes dipped in flaming paint. Usually they are herbs, but they may have perennial woody parts. They are root parasitic, meaning they get some nourishment by growing into the roots of other plants. They grow in hilly or mountainous areas, making bright spots of color. The flowers are tiny but grow in dense spikes, with the calyx and bracts the colored parts. The corolla is very small, inconspicuous and greenish, sometimes not even showing above the colored calyx. The upper lip of the corolla is long and narrow, enclosing the style and four unequal-length stamens. The lower lip is very short with three tiny teeth. The calyx and bracts may be broad and entire, or may be lobed or deeply divided. There are many species, often difficult to distinguish.

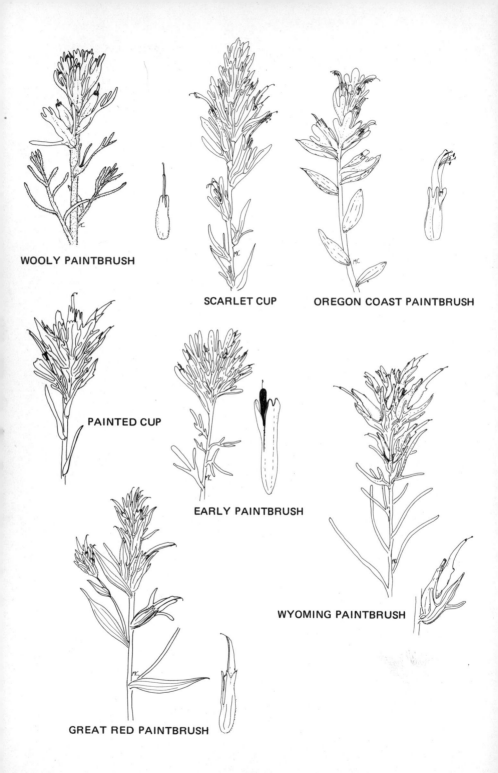

WOOLY PAINTBRUSH

SCARLET CUP

OREGON COAST PAINTBRUSH

PAINTED CUP

EARLY PAINTBRUSH

WYOMING PAINTBRUSH

GREAT RED PAINTBRUSH

Woolly Paintbrush, *Castilleja foliolosa,* has many stems, 10-18 inches (25-45 cm) high, from a woody base. The stems and narrow linear leaves are white-woolly. The bracts are three-parted, and the middle section is three-parted again. Both bracts and sepals are bright red-orange at the tip. Grows in California's Coast Ranges and western slopes of the Sierra Nevada to Lower California, 200-4,000 feet, blooming from March to June.

Scarlet Cup, Lay-and-Collies Paintbrush, *Castilleja affinis,* is hairy; the lanceolate leaves are rough. The bracts have two or three pairs of lobes tipped with bright red. The upper lip of the corolla is red-edged, the lower is dark green. It grows on dry brushy and wooded slopes throughout California's Coast Ranges, northern to southern California.

Oregon Coast Paintbrush, *Castilleja litoralis,* is found on sandy bluffs along the ocean and rocky coasts from Washington to northern California. The upper leaves are three-lobed and blunt. The bracts have a pair of short, roundish lobes. Both bracts and calyx are tipped in yellow or red.

Painted Cup, *Castilleja rhexifolia,* is the common paintbrush of the Rocky Mountain area, in the meadows or on cool, damp slopes. The bracts vary from creamy to deep purple-red in color. Both bracts and leaves are entire, not lobed.

Early Paintbrush, *Castilleja chromosa,* is an early paintbrush blooming from March on, depending on slope and elevation. Found in the Rocky Mountains from New Mexico north to Wyoming and Utah, west to Oregon and down its east side to eastern California, growing mainly on drier slopes. The bracts and sepals are vivid orange-red, the leaves are deeply cut, the bracts and sepals narrow.

Great Red Paintbrush, Indian Paintbrush, *Castilleja miniata,* is found in the mountains from 3,500-10,000 feet elevation in California, north to Alaska, east to Colorado, and through much of the Rockies. The flowers are thickly arranged at ends of branching stems 1-3 feet (30-90 cm) high, with the colored calyx and bract lobes deeply cut and appearing sharp. May be pink to purple to red; leaves mostly narrow and not hairy. Blooms from May to September.

Wyoming Paintbrush, *Castilleja linariaefolia,* is a common, brilliantly red, lovely paintbrush of the eastern Rockies and is the state flower of Wyoming. The leaves are narrow or grass-like or deeply divided. The bracts are deeply lobed, with very slender side lobes. The upper leaves and bracts are highly colored.

Owl's Flower, Owl's Clover, *Orthocarpus purpurascens,* is not a clover, in spite of a common name. In certain years, acres and acres of fields and hills are rose-purple with this "owl's face" flower; it is often found

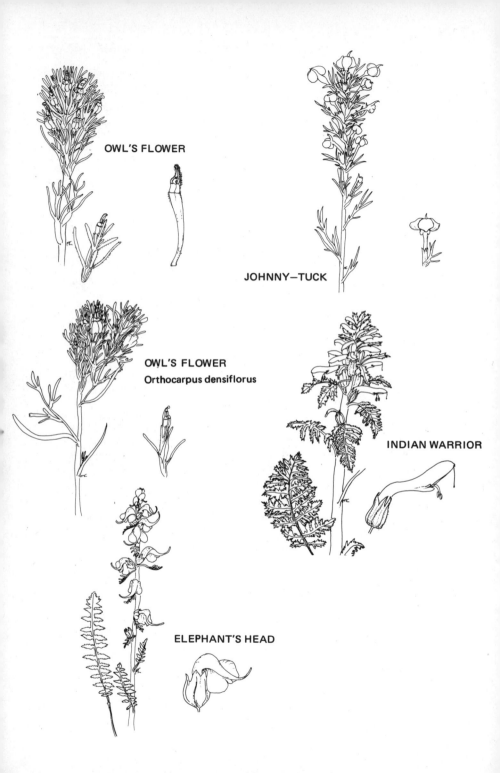

OWL'S FLOWER

JOHNNY—TUCK

OWL'S FLOWER
Orthocarpus densiflorus

INDIAN WARRIOR

ELEPHANT'S HEAD

abundantly among lupines and poppies, producing a fabulous pattern. White or cream-colored ones can be found also. The 4-15 inch (10-37.5 cm) plant has few branches. The 1 inch (2.5 cm) flowers vary from pale to deep rose-purple, with white tips and yellow and purple dots. Each flower in the closely packed spike has a lobed, pink-tipped bract at its base; calyx is also pink-tipped. The corolla is two-lipped, the upper lip curving and partly enclosing the slender style and stamens. The lower lip is slightly puffy and folded in, with three tiny teeth. Owl's flower is built much like the paintbrushes, but its lower lip is the large, longer one. The leaves are divided into very narrow segments and the upper ones may be pink-tipped; seeds are in a capsule.

Orthocarpus densiflorus is another common owl's flower, but is more slender though the spike is very dense. Bracts and sepals are purple-tipped with crimson spots on the lower lip, but not as brightly colored as *Orthocarpus purpurascens*. The three erect purple teeth are almost as tall as the upper lip. Both species are distributed widely over the West, blooming from March to May.

Johnny-Tuck, Butter and Eggs, *Orthocarpus erianthus*   It is easy to see that Johnny-Tuck is related to the paintbrushes and owl's flower, for the plants have the same general appearance of many colored bracts among small irregular flowers. The flowers of Johnny-Tuck are a light sulphur yellow. They often spread a solid carpet of color in patches on hillsides and valleys of California and southern Oregon from March to May. The flowers are about ¾ inch (1.8 cm) long, with a dark purple beak and a white corolla tube with two greenish yellow spots. The two upper petals are small, the three lower ones spread in sac-like shapes that seem inflated. The plant is branching, 4-10 inches (10-25 cm) tall, the spikes of flowers appearing flat-topped. The leaves, bracts and stems are purplish, especially near the flower tips.

Indian Warrior, *Pedicularis densiflora,* very attractive plant with a blending of reds, purples and wine-colors. They resemble the paintbrushes and owl's flower in shape, except the petals are more noticeable. The plant grows 9-24 inches (22.5-60 cm) tall. The corolla is crimson red, surrounded with long purplish-red hairy calyxes and greenish-red bracts. They make a bold splash of color, growing in the shade of oaks and shrubs on hillsides. They have large dark green leaves, which are deeply lobed and cut, tinged with brown and red. The leaves grow in a thick cluster from the base of the plants. Smaller leaves alternate up the purple flower stems. They bloom in the very early spring in California and Oregon.

Elephant Head, *Pedicularis groenlandica,* is a common flower found in the wet meadows of the high mountains all over the West, north to Canada, and east to Labrador. They are well-named, for each small pinkish or purplish flower is shaped much like the head of an elephant. The upper lip is bulbous, then narrows to a long beak which bends down over the lower

TOADFLAX

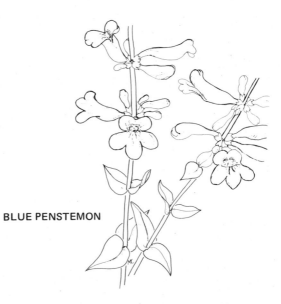

BLUE PENSTEMON

lip, and then upwards, resembling the elephant's trunk. The outer two lobes of the lower lip are large, and seem to be the elephant's ears. Many flowers are crowded into the spike on the leafy stalk from a basal clump. All the leaves are very finely divided and fern-like. Blooms from June on, even into late August in the high altitudes.

Toadflax, Butter and Eggs, *Linaria vulgaris,* is a slender snapdragon-like pale yellow flower particularly abundant along roadsides, fields, and meadows of the Rockies, westward to the coast, from low valleys to high elevations. The flowers grow in clusters at the end of stems. Often many flowering stems, 6-20 inches (15-50 cm) high, grow from the rest. The three-lobed yellow lower lip has an orange humped center and the upper lip lobes look like upright yellow "ears." The lower lip also has a 1 inch (2.5 cm) long pointed spur. The leaves are narrow, the lower ones 1½ inches (3.8 cm) long, progressively smaller up the stem. Blooms in July and August through much of the West.

PENSTEMON, Beard Tongue, all have two-lipped corollas with two-lobe upper lip and a three-lobe lower lip, the bases fused into a long tube. The name *Penstemon* means five stamens; all penstemons have five stamens, but only four of them have anthers. The fifth is always present, but has no anther, so produces no pollen. The fifth stamen is very noticeable, however. It is often very large, and is attached to the base of the lower lip, usually curving to lie against its lobes at the throat opening. Sometimes it is bushy or hairy at the tip and serves as a "pollen duster" with visiting insects. Beard tongue as a common name was given this group because of the hairy fifth stamen. The other four stamens are arranged in pairs, attached by their filaments to the base of the upper lip, the filaments curving to fit the shape of the corolla. The calyx is small, showing the plan of five by its tips. The style usually is inconspicuous amid the stamens. The capsule, often quite pointed, holds many seeds. The leaves are always opposite, with the upper ones sessile or clasping. They vary in type and may be smooth or notched. Penstemons are among the most beautiful and showy of all wildflowers, with their long clusters of bright, large flowers. They may be white, pink, red, lavender to deep blue and purple. They grow in many types of area—desert to high mountains and are native to North America. Many have been developed for choice garden flowers. Wild species are favorite foods of wild sheep, marmots, etc.

Blue Penstemon, *Penstemon cyananthus,* the most beautiful of all wild penstemons, grows from 5,000-9,000 feet elevation in the Rocky Mountains. This is a fabulous deep blue flower, with the throat often purplish or light blue, sometimes even pinkish. The many showy blossoms grow in whorls along the stem. It grows 1-2 feet (30-60 cm) tall, and has smooth glossy green opposite clasping leaves. They form brilliant masses of color on new road cuts or in rocky fields and meadows, often with paintbrush and columbine.

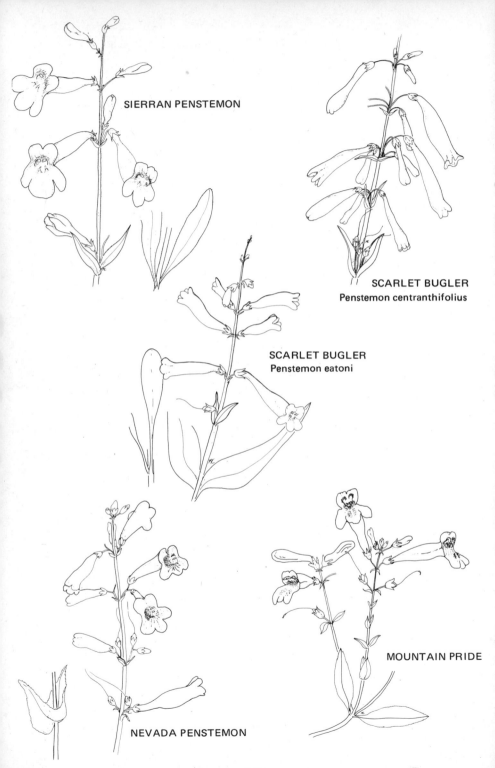

SIERRAN PENSTEMON

SCARLET BUGLER
Penstemon centranthifolius

SCARLET BUGLER
Penstemon eatoni

NEVADA PENSTEMON

MOUNTAIN PRIDE

158

Sierran Penstemon, *Penstemon laetus,* grows on dry rocky wooded or chaparral areas from the southern Sierra along the western slope of the Sierra Nevada to southern Oregon and east to Nevada. The blossoms vary in color from blue to purple to pink. There are two white patches on the throat of the lower lip. The corolla tube is about 1 inch (2.5 cm) long, with two white anthers showing; stamens may be tinged with purple. The five lobes spread far apart, leaving the throat wide open. The opposite leaves are narrow, entire, and sessile all along the stem. The plants have a woody base with stems up to 14 inches (35 cm) long.

Scarlet Bugler, *Penstemon centranthifolius*   The bright, flaming vermillion tubes of scarlet bugler are very noticeable. They grow on dry hillsides, cliffs, or sandy places from central California, south into the deserts and east into Colorado, Arizona, and Utah. The panicle of blossoms grow on slender stems 1-4 feet (30-120 cm) tall. The pedicel is long and slender so each flower is a hanging fiery red tube about 1 inch (2.5 cm) long, with five nearly equal, narrow lobes. These turn backward in sets of two and three, forming two-lips. The leaves are opposite, smooth, and rather thick; upper ones are sessile. They bloom from April to June, from 600-4,700 feet elevation.

Penstemon eatoni is very similar to *Penstemon centranthifolius,* growing in desert areas of California, Arizona, Nevada, and Utah, and is also called scarlet bugler. The bright scarlet tubular flowers are shorter but more two-lipped and the stems are purplish.

Nevada Penstemon, *Penstemon pseudospectabilis,* is a very big-flowered, tall-growing, 2-5 feet (60-150 cm), succulent, gray-leafed Penstemon growing along dry roadsides and roadcuts especially in southern California, Nevada, and Arizona. The flowers are often larger than garden snapdragons, varying from almost white to deep pink, with many conspicuous lines on the lower lip. The throat of the corolla opens widely, showing the two pairs of stamens with horseshoe shaped anthers curling against the upper lip and the sterile stamen with its golden yellow brush lying against the lower lip. The plant is beautiful even when not in bloom because of the large basal clump of big, toothed, gray leaves.

Mountain Pride, *Penstemon newberryi,* is the low common red penstemon, varying from deep pink crimson or pink-purple to bright red. It is found on rocky ledges, 4,000-10,000 feet, all over California into Oregon. It forms dense, low clumps especially in granite areas. The corolla is 1-1½ inches (2.5-3.8 cm) long, with the upper lip standing upright and a patch of white hairs on the lower lip. A distinguishing characteristic is that the stamens stand outward or project, not fitting the corolla tightly as in many species; the anthers are white-woolly: the calyx is sticky. As in many Penstemons, the style persists on the mature capsules. *Penstemon rupicala,* with rose-purple, nearly red or deep pink flowers, is quite similar. It is found in northern California to central Washington. The stamens do not project as far and the plant forms a more compact mat.

MATILIJA POPPY

Chapter X

FLOWERS WITH MORE
THAN FIVE PETALS

Thousands of flowers in the world seem to have more than five petals; however, only a few really have more than five *true* petals. Most "many-petalled" flowers will be Composites, like daisies, which are described in the next chapter. Some may be Lilies or Iris which seem to have six petals.

The majority of flowers with "six petals" really have three sepals and three petals, colored alike but actually forming two circles. The three in the outside circle are really sepals and enclose the three in the inner circle, which are the petals. Most of these flowers belong to the Lily or Iris Families (see chapter IV), are built on the plan of three and have parallel-veined leaves.

There is no one family which characteristically has more than five petals, but there are a few flowers in two or three different families that do. Some members of the Poppy Family have more than five petals, and when they do the number of petals is twice the number of sepals. The California buttercup in the Buttercup Family has many petals (usually eight to thirteen), as does bitterroot in the Purslane Family. There are some others in the world; we have included only these.

POPPY FAMILY
Papaveraceae

Matilija Poppy, *Romneya coulteri,* is one of the most striking members of the lovely Poppy Family. They are abundant near the Grand Canyon, and are found blooming in late spring or summer in dry parts of the Southwest and into Mexico. Where there is enough moisture, they sometimes grow 6-7 feet (180-210 cm) tall on strong prickly stems, forming a large, spreading bush-like plant with gray-green, divided leaves. The blossoms resemble huge single peonies, sometimes 6-9 inches (15-22.5 cm) across. They have six lovely, crinkled white petals and, as is characteristic with the Poppy Family, three sepals (the number of petals is twice the number of sepals). The sepals are smooth and remain on after the flower blooms, instead of falling as in many Poppies. The cluster of orange-yellow stamens surround the light green pistil. The superior ovary develops into a many-seeded capsule.

THISTLE POPPY

CREAM CUPS

CALIFORNIA BUTTERCUP

Thistle Poppy, Prickly Poppy, *Argemone platyceras* var. *hispida,* is similar
to matilija poppy, but the plant is hairy and prickly with long yellow
spines, grows 1½-5 feet (45-150 cm) high, with leaves 2-9 inches
(5-22.5 cm) long. The large white six-petal blossoms are arranged in leafy
panicles. Each of the three sepals has a horn at the apex. Thistle poppy
blooms in the late spring through summer in the Coast Ranges, southern
California, the Southwest, east to Texas.

Cream Cups, *Platystemon californicum,* are lovely cream-colored wildflowers which often grow in such masses that the field appears frosted
with whipped cream. They grow abundantly in grassy valley and foothill
areas of California, Oregon, and Arizona. Often they are mistaken for pale
buttercups, but these have three sepals (not five as Buttercups), and six
petals (not five as many Buttercups or eight to thirteen as California
buttercups). The petals are pale cream and not glossy and waxy as are
Buttercups. The three sepals are hairy and enclose a nodding bud. As the
bud opens into a flower, it turns upward as a cup, the sepals dropping off.
Each plant produces many hairy flower stems, with the hairy leaves
clustered at the base. The filaments of some inner stamens are quite broad.
The compound pistil has many styles, each connected to its part in the
superior ovary. Many seeds develop, appearing like strings of little beads,
and then many "strings of beads" twist together. This pistil is not a
collection of separate pistils, as in Buttercups, nor as united as in other
members of the Poppy Family.

BUTTERCUP FAMILY
Ranunculaceae

California Buttercup, *Ranunculus californicus,* is another of the
many unusual members of the Buttercup Family, because it has more
than five true petals. This family has not established dependable
patterns of number of parts, which is a sign of its primitive character.
California buttercup is so undependable that the number of petals
varies from eight to thirteen, sometimes right on the same plant.

It is very common in moist valleys, hillsides, and roadsides of
California, Oregon, and Washington. Sometimes it colors whole
swampy or moist fields and slopes golden yellow. This slender
branching plant, 9-18 inches (22.5-45 cm) high, produces many
glossy blossoms, each one at the tip of a branch. The five sepals fold
back on themselves. There are many stamens, and the numerous
pistils cluster on a mound. Each pistil develops into a small hooked
achene. The bright green leaves are deeply divided and very characteristic of this species, usually 1-3 inches (2.5-7.5 cm) long, though
the basal leaves may be longer. Indians browned the seeds over the
fire to remove their bitter flavor, then ground them to use as flour.

BITTERROOT

PURSLANE FAMILY
Portulacaceae

Bitterroot, Redhead Louisa, *Lewisia rediviva,* is very common in the northern Rockies, but extends south into Utah and west into northern California. It is the state flower of Montana, and is expecially abundant in the western part of that state. It was first collected by an early botanist on the Lewis and Clark Expedition and was named for Meriweather Lewis.

It may confuse you as to its family, but it does fit the general pattern of Purslane. The small succulent leaves appear as the snows melt or weather warms and are often withered and gone when the pink or whitish, many-petaled flower blooms. The flower is 1-2 inches (2.5-5 cm) across on a 1-3 inch (2.5-7.5 cm) stem growing from a fleshy root-crown. There are six to eight petal-like sepals, twelve to eighteen petals, and many stamens. The filaments of the stamens are united at their bases and there are six to eight styles. Another species, *Lewisia pygmaea,* has flowers which resemble spring beauty (see page 80). This Lewisia has six to eight petals and a two-cleft style.

The flower is beautiful, though it withers quickly. The importance of the plant as a food for early people (Indians, explorers, and settlers) makes it a good choice for a state flower. The root is fleshy and full of stored starch, especially before the blossoms use it up. It is bitter until it is cooked. The Indians located it in the early spring by its leaves. The outside layer of the root peels off easily and the inside is white and fleshy. They baked, boiled, or powdered it for meal. Indians in Montana and Idaho still gather it.

The plant, if dug and dried, will still grow when replanted many weeks later. It is found all over the Rocky Mountains, westward to British Columbia and south through the mountains to the central portion of the Sierra and Coast Ranges of California.

Chapter XI

FLOWERS THAT SEEM
TO HAVE MANY PETALS

These flowers seem to have many petals, but are not included in Chapter X because only flowers with many true petals are included there. Flowers in this chapter are *Composite* or compounded of many distinct flowers grouped tightly together at the end of the stems, so that all together they seem to be one big blossom. It is very important to examine them carefully to see the separate flowers. Once you learn the characteristics, it is easy to recognize them as a distinct group, even though there is much variety.

SUNFLOWER FAMILY
Compositae

This is the largest flower family; its 10,000 species are found all over the world. The flowers are extremely specialized for the job of producing seeds. The "flower" is not a single flower, but a collection of flowers in a tight head on a large receptable, surrounded by an involucre. A spike of flowers, with all the flowers pushed to the top, surrounded by the leaves also pushed up, would be similar to a Composite. Each part of the head is typically a tiny complete flower with a calyx, a five-tooth corolla with five attached stamens and a style that is two-part. The calyx is modified into a papery or hairy calyx called a pappus.

Each "petal" is really a single flower, called the "ray flower." They are specialized to advertise and attract pollinating insects. The corolla is often large and becomes one-sided so that, along with the many other ray flowers, it makes a circle of color around a center. The ray flowers may have just stamens or just pistils, or sometimes neither. The "center" of the flower may be made up of many tiny "disc flowers." The corolla is small and inconspicuous, but a magnifying glass shows its five-toothed upper edge. The five sta-

SUNFLOWER

ROCKY MOUNTAIN SUNFLOWER

mens form a tight collar around the style and they typically produce much pollen. Each flower has a one-cell inferior ovary. Sunflower "seeds" are examples of these simple ovaries, the center of the sunflower being a tightly packed collection of dozens of separate disc flowers. The disc flowers are the main seed producers. Gaillardias (page 177) are excellent flowers to show the general characteristics.

The Sunflower family is divided into twelve tribes to help make identification easier. We will not give details of the tribes, but since there are three types of flower heads, we will group them this way:

    1. Daisy-like flowers with both ray and disc flowers.

    2. Thistle-like flowers with only disc flowers, but the lobes of the tubular corolla are often long; the involucral bracts may be spiny.

    3. Dandelion-like flowers with only ray flowers; typically make a large seed head when the tiny flowers mature.

In most Composites, the pappus helps in distribution, as the down of a thistle.

1. DAISY-LIKE FLOWERS: BOTH RAY AND DISC FLOWERS

Sunflower, *Helianthus annuus,* are shaped like daisies, but usually are large and most species are yellow. The common sunflower in valleys of the West, familiar to most Americans, is *Helianthus annuus* which was introduced from the Great Plains many years ago where it grows from Minnesota to Texas. It is the state flower of Kansas. The clear yellow ray petals surround the dark disc flowers. Each flower head is 3-5 inches (7.5-12.5 cm) across, growing alone on the end of a branching stem. This species has been improved and grown in gardens and fields for its seeds. Cultivated sunflowers may have heads a foot (30 cm) across, and develop large seeds useful for chicken feed, or ground into a meal from which cakes of cattle feed are made; seeds are also used for oil and roasted and eaten as nuts. Indians gathered the wild seeds for food, to make purple and black dye. and used the oil to grease their hair. Now sunflowers are grown all over the world, especially in Mexico and Russia.

Rocky Mountain Sunflower, *Helianthus nuttallii,* fills whole grassy meadows and warm spots along streams with its bright yellow flowers. Both its ray and disc flowers are yellow, the flowers smaller than the midwestern species, usually 2-4 inches (5-10 cm) across, growing on the ends of slender, *unbranched* stems. However, there are many 2-3 foot (60-90 cm) stems growing from each leafy clump. The leaves are opposite on the lower part of the stem, alternate on the upper.

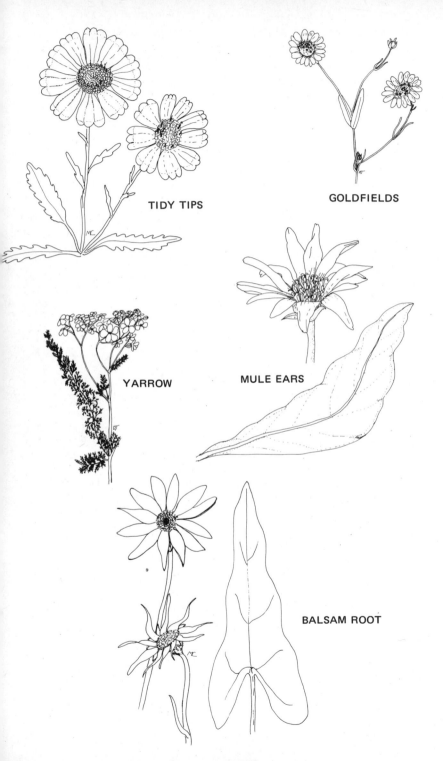

TIDY TIPS

GOLDFIELDS

YARROW

MULE EARS

BALSAM ROOT

Tidy Tips, *Layia platyglossa*   This daisy-like flower is 1½ inches (3.8 cm) across, with white tips on the yellow ray flowers. It carpets valleys and hills from 100-4,600 feet elevation, throughout California and on the southwestern desert. They often grow among cream cups and goldfields. The plants are 4-16 inches (10-40 cm) high, depending on the moisture. The bracts are sepal-like. The ray flowers have no stamens; disc flowers are complete. The tubular corolla of the disc flower is shorter than the anther-collar and style. The seed is small, topped by calyx (pappus) bristles. It flowers in March and April.

Goldfields, *Baeria chrysostoma,* is appropriately named for sometimes great fields of many acres are golden with this tiny flower. Both plant and blossom are tiny in dry fields, but larger when rain is plentiful; sometimes they are no more than 2 inches (5 cm) high. The flowers are daisy-like with five to fifteen conspicuous ray flowers with pistils only, and as many bracts as there are ray flowers. The disc flowers are very tiny and crowded. They are a darker yellow. The opposite, light green leaves are covered with fine hairs and grow on slender stems. Bloom in March and April in most of California.

Yarrow, Milfoil, *Achillea millefolium*   These perennial plants have such finely divided leaves that they resemble ferns. They grow alternately and are hairy and slightly sticky. The many stems grow 1-3 feet (30-90 cm) tall, each with a flattopped cluster of tiny blossom heads. There usually are only five white ray flowers; the very tiny disc flowers are yellow. Both types of flowers are complete, but with practically no calyx. Yarrow grows in Europe and came to America from there; now it grows all over Canada and the U.S. It blooms in March and April in California, in June to September in most of America. There are garden species.

Mule-ears, *Wyethia helenioides*   The large leaves of mule-ears are about the shape and size of a mule's ear, so this is a good name for the plant. They are 1-2 feet (30-60 cm) long, 4-6 inches (10-15 cm) wide, velvety when young, becoming stiff, smooth, and dark green as they age. They are mostly basal. The large sunflower-like blossoms make this sturdy plant very showy. They are about 3 inches (7.5 cm) across, growing on stems 1-2 feet (30-60 cm) tall. This species has twelve to eighteen yellow ray flowers. Various species grow from Colorado to the Pacific.

Wyethia glabra, also called mule-ears, is common in the West. Its leaves are sticky but hairless and there are usually fifteen large yellow ray flowers with both pistils and stamens. They grow in the interior valley, on Sierran and coastal hills of California, blooming in March and April.

Balsam Root, *Balsamrhiza sagittata,* forms big clumps with many flower stems 1-2 feet (30-60 cm) high, from the large basal leaves. These arrowhead-shaped leaves haVe long stems and appear gray-white because of thick hair. The flowers are somewhat like small gold-yellow sunflow-

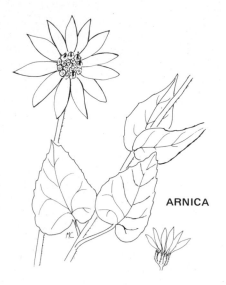

ARNICA

BLOW WIVES

ers, coloring acres when in bloom, but individual flowers wither soon and
the ray flowers drop off. Indians used the young shoots, seeds, and roots
for food. It is an important range plant for animals, both domesticated and
wild. It grows abundantly on dry open hills and mountain sides, British
Columbia south through the Rockies and east to the Black Hills.

Balsamrhiza hookeri, another balsamroot, has bigger, yellower flowers and
can easily be distinguished, for its foliage is green, not gray-hairy, and the
large leaves are pinnately divided and cleft. The range is similar.

Arnica, *Arnica cordifolia*   There are several similar species of arnicas in
the West; the flowers resemble mule-ears and balsamroot, but both leaves
and flowers are smaller. There are many yellow disc flowers that are often
darker than the ray flowers; the ray flowers are pistillate; the involucre
bracts are large. The bright clumps with many flowering stems are very
noticeable along roadsides and meadows in the mountains of the West.
The leaves are somewhat heart-shaped. This species grows from creeping
rootstocks, stems 6-24 inches (15-60 cm) high. Found from
4,000-10,000 feet, California north to British Columbia, east to Colorado
and south to Arizona and New Mexico.

Blow-wives, *Achyrachaena mollis,* usually is not noticed until it goes to
seed, for then it forms a large white head with the pappus looking like ten
parchment "petals." The head is narrow, the white flowers tipped with
reddish-brown and held in and almost hidden by long thin bracts. Each
bract encloses one of the five to eight short pistillate ray flowers. The disc
flowers are complete but narrow and tubular, almost as tall as the ray
flowers. The narrow downy leaves are about 5 inches (12.5 cm) long,
growing alternately up the 9-19 inch (22.-45 cm) tall plants. The black
"seeds" are carried in the wind by the pappus. Grows in adobe soil all
over California valleys and hills up to 2,600 feet, and into southern
Oregon, blooming in late spring.

ASTER   There are many Asters in the West, all very similar to
those found throughout the United States. The slender ray flowers
may be white, pink, blue, or violet. The disc flowers are yellow,
sometimes turning to red, brown, or purple as they age. Usually they
grow with many blossoms in a raceme at the ends of slender stems on
a many-branched plant, but a few Asters have single heads to a stem.
There are several series of bracts, the outer ones usually shorter and
smaller. The stems are leafy, the leaves alternate and simple. Most of
them are late summer or fall blooming herbs. If you know one, you
probably can identify all others as Asters, though the genus Erigeron
(page 00) is quite similar and confusing, and several asters have been
regrouped recently under the genus *Machaeranthera.*

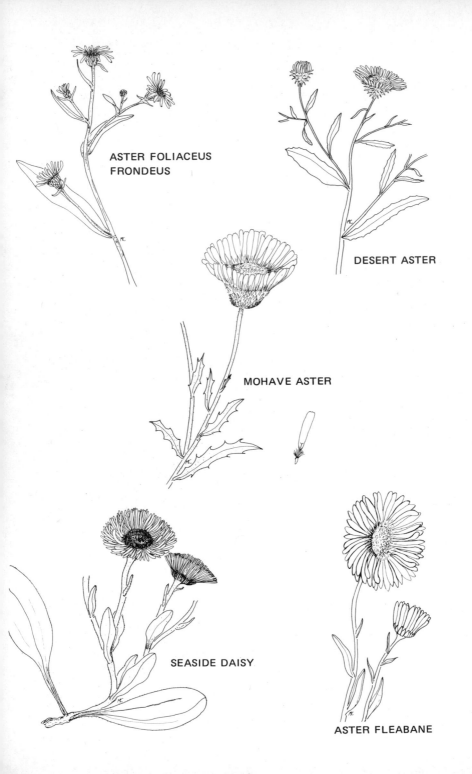

ASTER FOLIACEUS
FRONDEUS

DESERT ASTER

MOHAVE ASTER

SEASIDE DAISY

ASTER FLEABANE

Aster foliaceus frondeus, the tall leafy bract Aster, is a much-branched, many-flowered plant of valley, field, and roadside of the West, the plant growing 1-2½ feet (30-75 cm) high, with the lavender flowers ½-1 inch (1.3-2.5 cm) across, each at the tip of the much-branched raceme. Many are in bloom at the same time, so the plant has dozens of little lavender, yellow-centered flowers scattered over the top. There usually are fifteen to twenty slender pistillate ray flowers and fifteen to twenty-five small disc flowers. The leaves are lance-shaped, smooth-edged, clasping and extending all along the stems. It blooms from August to late September in California, north into British Columbia and east to Colorado.

Desert Aster   Many Asters grow in the deserts of the West: In California, Arizona, and Utah deserts, *Aster tephrodes* is an amethyst blue species with twenty-five to forty ray flowers in the head, blooming from April to October, growing on dry, rocky hillsides and along the roadsides; *Aster tanacetifolius* is the species most commonly found in the Texas deserts. This bright violet Aster, blooms from June to October; Mojave Aster *Machaeranthera tortifolia,* is the most common species in California deserts, but also abundant in southwestern Utah and northwestern Arizona. The forty to sixty ray flowers of this species are amethyst blue to almost white, the leaves sharply toothed. California desert aster blooms from March through May, and often again in October.

Aster Daisy, Aster Fleabane, *Erigeron peregrinus* var. *salsuginosus,* resembles Aster, but there are only one or two rows of neatly arranged bracts in the involucre. Usually there are many slender ray flowers in this genus. *Erigerons* do not grow very tall, usually less than 1½ feet (45 cm). The very beautiful, large, deep-lavender flower has many yellow disc flowers and thirty to fifty slender ray flowers, each with a tiny notch in the tip. The flower is 1½-2 inches (3.8-5 cm) across. The bract tips spread or curve downwards. The plant grows from a thick rootstalk about a foot (30 cm) high, usually not branched, or with only one or two branches near the top. The leaves are alternate, largest are 2 inches (5 cm) long. It is a common flower of high mountain meadows 5,000-10,000 feet in the Rockies, north to Alaska, south to New Mexico, west to British Columbia and south through Oregon and Washington mountains to the Sierra Nevada.

Seaside Daisy, *Erigeron glaucus,* is characteristic of the seacoast area from Oregon south to Monterey County in central California. Several stiff stems grow 4-10 inches (10-25 cm) high from a root-crown of woody prostrate branches with basal leaves. Leaves are 1-4 inches (2.5-10 cm) long with smaller upper leaves. The flower heads are 1-1½ inches (2.5-3.8 cm) across, with many (about a hundred) narrow ray flowers which may be lilac to white in color. Common on sandy stretches or coastal cliffs, blooming from May to August.

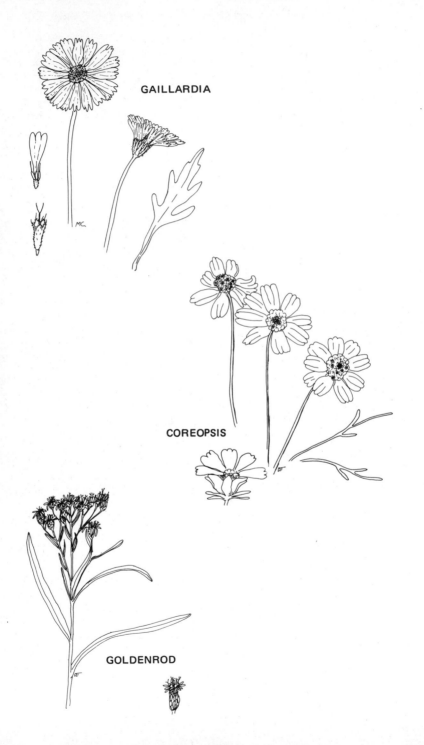

GAILLARDIA

COREOPSIS

GOLDENROD

Gaillardia, Blanketflower, *Gaillardia aristata, Gaillardia arizonica,* are excellent flowers to study as typical Composites for the ray and disc flowers are complete and large. The huge blossoms of Gaillardia are so attractive that they are noticed wherever they grow. The great-flowered gaillardia, *Gaillardia aristata,* is common in the Northwest, especially along the Columbia River, extending as far east as Montana and North Dakota, north into Canada. The plant is 1-3 feet (30-90 cm) tall, has many stems, and sometimes has flowers as large as 4 inches (10 cm) across. The disc flowers are orange to red-purple, with the ray flowers yellow or shading at their bases to orange or purple or brown. The receptacles of all Gaillardias are covered with stiff hairs. This species has been improved and grown in gardens, many times escaping back to the wild.

The Arizona Gaillardia, *Gaillardia arizonica,* is much smaller, only 4-8 inches (10-20 cm) tall, bearing a single flower about 2 inches (5 cm) across. The ray flowers are golden yellow with three teeth. The disc flowers are shaded from deep maroon to yellow, turning to a purplish, fuzzy, round head when the rays drop. The plants have rough, hairy stiff stalks and leaves. This species can be found as a summer flower in dry areas as far west as southern California.

Coreopsis, *Coreopsis douglasii*   There are different kinds of coreopsis growing all over the world, most of them a lovely clear yellow, but a small rose-colored one grows in swampy areas along the Atlantic. Most western species are perennial. The involucre is double, with the lower or outer row of bracts holding the cup-like upper portion. The leaves are divided into narrow lobes. Each of the long, naked stems produces a single yellow flower with three-toothed ray flowers about 1 inch (2.5 cm) long. In some species the base of the rays is brown. The disc flowers are very tightly packed onto a nearly flat receptacle with thin bracts which fall off with the fruit. The pappus is a tiny corky ring or cup which makes the achene look enough like a bug to give the plant its scientific name meaning "bug-like." This species blooms in the spring in valleys and mesa areas of central California, south to Lower California east to Arizona, and south to Mexico.

Goldenrod, *Solidago californica,* grows as a tall spray of deep yellow flowers along roads and in fields in late summer. The sprays are made of many slender branches carrying dozens of small daisy-like flowers, each about ⅛ inch (.3 cm) across. They have seven to twelve tiny ray flowers and a center of five to twelve disc flowers. The whole spray makes an attractive "golden rod" against the drying grasses of late summer and fall. The plant may grow 1-4 feet (30-120 cm) high, branched part way up the main stem into two to four erect divisions. Leaves are alternate, lance-shaped with a few teeth and a prominent midrib, grayish underneath. As the ovaries mature, each flower head becomes a mass of long white hairs formed from the pappus. This species is found in California and Oregon.

There are many similar species all over the United States; Alabama,

TAR WEED

YELLOW STAR THISTLE

Kentucky, and Nebraska have goldenrod as their state flower. Western goldenrod, *Solidago occidentalis,* is a common species of the Rocky Mountain area, west to British Columbia and south to California. It grows 3-5 feet (30-150 cm) high, with leafy branches. The leaves have tiny dark or light resinous spots. The flowers grow all around the stem, while a similar one, *Solidago elongata,* has the tiny flowers arranged on just the upper side of each branch.

Tar Weed, *Hemizonia virgata*   These annuals have sticky smelly, gray-green leaves and branches. The leaves are narrow, usually alternate, on a 1-1½ foot (30-45 cm) plant. There are many heads made of four to seven creamy or greenish ray flowers and seven to ten disc flowers with black stamens bearing white anthers. Often entire fields in dry valleys and low hills are white from July to October all over the West with this flower.

Coast tar weed, *Madia sativa,* has large yellow or white flower heads. The nutritious oil pressed from the seeds of this plant is made into cakes for cattle feed and used as a cooking oil. Indians gathered the seeds and ground them into a meal which they ate dry. They also made soap from the oil of the seeds and used the blossoms to cure poison oak.

2. THISTLE-LIKE: DISC FLOWERS ONLY

The most familiar members of this group of Composites are the common thistles. Some species are very lovely, most of them are showy, but many are considered real pests because they become terrible weeds. They are prolific in their seed production, the seeds are carried readily by wind or animals, and some species spread by underground roots. The prickles on leaves and involucres give them the common name of knights-in-armor.

Thistles have flower heads made up of tube-shaped disc flowers only. The lobes of the corollas are usually long and slender. All thistles have small ''seeds'' which are carried in the wind by their hairy tip of fluff, or by hooks which catch in fur and are carried by animals. The thistle is the national emblem of Scotland. Some garden flowers that belong in the thistle group are bachelor's button and corn flower. Young, peeled flower stems can be eaten like celery; the down of the seed is useful for fire tinder.

Yellow Star Thistle, Barnaby Thistle, *Centaurea solstitialis,* is a small bright yellow prickly branching annual thistle found along roads, in waste areas, and fields over much of the West, particularly in valleys up to mid altitudes. The brilliant shiny yellow corollas of the tiny disc flowers are tubular and divided into long lobes. The involucral bracts surrounding the round flower heads have prickles ½-¾ inch (1.3-1.8 cm) long and the upper bracts are winged. These shiny bracts help give it the name yellow star thistle. The shiny wings become hard, the prickles persist, and the plant dries to form a whitish prickly tangle.

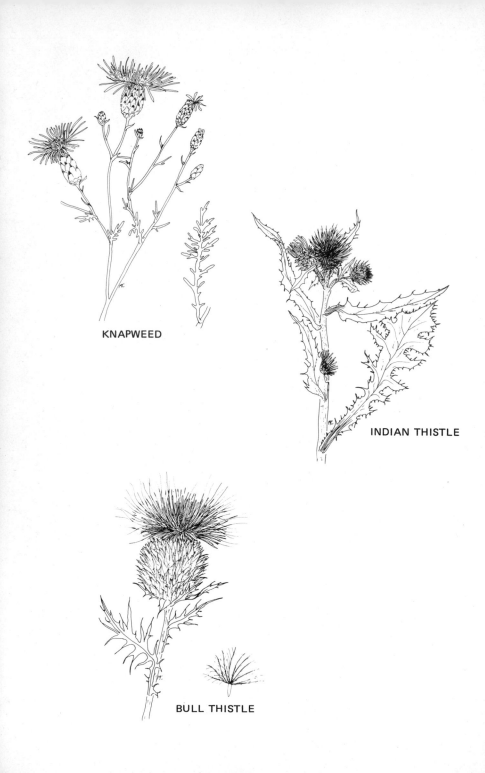

KNAPWEED

INDIAN THISTLE

BULL THISTLE

It grows 12-18 inches (30-45 cm) tall with small leaves along its stiff slender branches. The leaves are not spiny edged in this group of thistles, but are attached by their midrib along the stem for part of their length, giving the stem a winged or angled appearance. The basal leaves are divided; leaves and stems are covered with gray cottony hairs. This terrible weed, especially in grain fields, was introduced from Europe and is spreading and ruining much valuable agricultural and grazing land. It begins to bloom near the time of the summer solstice, which gives it the species name.

Knapweed, *Centaurea maculosa*   Whole fields of this late-summer, early-fall wildflower are to be found in Idaho, western Montana, Oregon, and northern California from July to September. Your first thought is that the field or roadside is a mass of lavender asters, but when looked at closely, you realize it is not an aster, since there aren't both ray and disc flowers.

This native of Europe is now very common in the East and is spreading westward. The plant is many-branched, 1-3 feet (30-90 cm) high, with the lower leaves considerably larger than the upper ones. All the leaves show such deep divisions that at first glance you think they are simple, very narrow leaves; they are not at all prickly. Many flowers are on each branch, blooming from the tip first. They are of a clear lavender-pink, with the head held at the base by a vase-shaped collection of bracts. Each bract has a black tip, giving the involucre a spotted appearance. The tiny flowers are numerous, twenty-five to fifty per head. The pollen matures early, then the long slender pistil grows out beyond the circle of stamens.

From a distance it may resemble Canada thistle, but the mass doesn't seem as dense because the leaves are so finely divided. Also, of course, the Canada thistle has very prickly leaves and larger seed heads than the knapweed. Canada thistle tends to be a slender plant with the flower heads in flattopped clusters.

Indian Thistle, *Cirsium edule,* is a common, tall, biennial, prickly stemmed, prickly leafed thistle of the lands along the Pacific Ocean, Canada to Lower California. The corollas are dull purple to pink to whitish. The leafy stem is straight with few branches, 3-6 feet (1-2 m) tall. The leaves are long 8-10 inches (20-25 cm) and thick, with cleft edges and prickles on the margins. There are several thistle heads in each terminal leafy cluster. The involucre is cobweb-woolly when the flower is new. Grows mainly in gulches or gravelly slopes at 50-1,500 feet elevation.

Bull Thistle,*Cirsium vulgare*   This common purple biennial thistle, introduced from Eurasia is now established over most of North America. It grows 2-5 feet (50-150 cm) tall with many spiny branches. The involucre is very prickly and is very noticeable since it is vase-shaped and not surrounded by leaves. The leaves are deeply cut and spiny-edged; the spines are yellowish. The upper side is covered with stiff hairs and a spiny ridge runs from the base of each leaf, along the stem to the next leaf. This

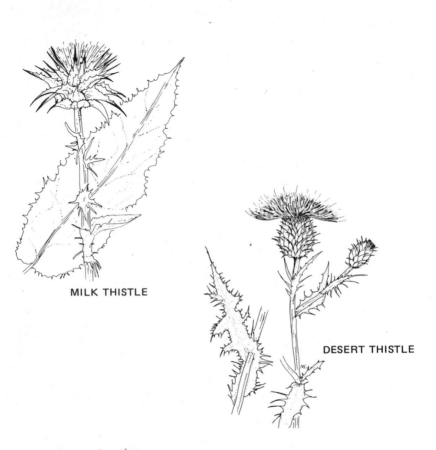

MILK THISTLE

DESERT THISTLE

CANADA THISTLE

is a distinguishing characteristic. The "seeds" are wind-carried by their thistledown, and each has a spongy ring that breaks and releases the seed when it absorbs water.

It likes fairly moist areas in fields and along roads, low elevations to 8,000 feet, all over the country, blooming from late June to September. A terrible weed.

Milk Thistle, *Silybum marianum,* is the commonest purple thistle of California. It shows much white in spots and along the veins of the very large, 12-18 inches (30-45 cm) long by 6-12 inches (15-30 cm) wide, prickly, notched leaves. These leaves identify the plant even before it blooms. It grows 3-6 feet (1-2 cm) tall and may branch many times. The heads are large, 2 inches (5 cm) across, with spines on the bracts 1-1½ inches (2.5-3.9 cm) long. Each of the tiny individual purple corollas is tubular with a bulge just below the long lobes. As in many thistles in bloom, the head appears frosty with the styles and pollen. Milk thistle takes over along roadsides, old fields and hillside spots, though early cutting before blooming can control it. It produces many airborne seeds and blooms May-July.

Desert Thistle, Mojave Thistle, *Cirsium mohavense,* is the most comomon thistle of southern California, into Nevada and Utah. The stout stem is 2-4 feet (30-60 cm) high with many branches at the top, each with its thistle head of reddish-to-pink-to-white flower heads, 1½ inches (3.8 cm) long. The straw-colored involucral bracts are each tipped with a long yellow spine. Basal leaves have petioles; mid leaves are sessile with spiny ridges running down the stem. Found in gravelly valleys, rocky slopes, or alkaline meadows at 2,000-6,000 feet.

Canada Thistle, *Cirsium arvense,* a small lavender thistle, is a terrific weed of the Northwest and Canada, growing 1-5 feet (30-150 cm) tall, forming dense patches along roads, into pastures and fields. The stems and leaves are spiny. The leaves are 2-4 inches (5-10 cm) wide. The flower head is quite small, 1 inch (2.5 cm) across, with the involucre urn-shaped and not particularly prickly, the bracts quite small and not bristle-tipped. The flower quickly goes to seed, the heads staying more or less together for awhile so they appear as dirty white, silky masses.

The plant resembles knapweed (page 180), *Centaurea maculosa,* in general appearance and flower color, though they may be a bit deeper lavender, but these have prickly, larger leaves which make the growth appear dense, not open, as in knapweed. Canada thistle spreads rapidly by abundant hairy seed masses, but also spreads by deep underground rootstocks over a 20-foot (6 m) radius. They are extremely hard to get rid of if they ever get started. Their needs for lots of water keeps them from spreading to drier regions of the country.

PINEAPPLE WEED

flower

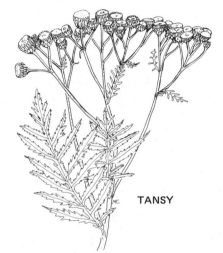

TANSY

WESTERN CONE FLOWER

COMMON PEARLY EVERLASTING

pistillate   staminate
flower   flower

184

Pineapple Weed, *Matricaria sauveolens,* a small weed, often carpets road-sides and fields with greenish-yellow. The many tiny disc flowers grow in a cone-shaped head, shaped somewhat like a pineapple. They have a strong fruity odor, too. The plants are small with feathery leaves. This is one of the early spring plants of the West.

Tansy, *Tanacetum vulgare,* a wildflower or "weed" as many Idahoans and Montanans prefer to think of it, grows in great masses of deep yellow, standing 3-4 feet (90-120 cm) high. The flower heads are made up of thirty to fifty little dome-shaped golden discs, very similar to brass buttons found in semi-swampy places. Each flower head is made of tightly packed disc flowers—hundreds of them. The whole flower head is also dome-shaped, not flat as in yarrow. The leaves are finely divided, fern-like in appearance, and alternately arranged on the stiff, tall stems, gradually decreasing in size as they approach the top. It becomes a pest in gardens and pastures, increasing rapidly. Makes masses of color along roadsides, often with knapweed (page 180) which is so common in the Northwest.

Rayless Coneflower, Western Coneflower, *Rudbeckia occidentalis,* or black-eyed Susans are common in the Rockies and the eastern part of the United States and are well-known garden plants. The western coneflower is unusual for it has no ray flowers, so is noticed as a tall plant, 3-6 feet (1-2 m), branching two or three times near the top, each branch producing a dark brown cone-shaped head on a naked stem. This cone may be 1-2½ inches (2.5-6 cm) high and 1 inch (2.5 cm) in diameter; it is made of closely packed dark tubular disc flowers only, and has a simple involucre below it. The flowers are striking, especially in aspen meadows along the tall lupines, often filling the meadow. The plant is leafy below the heads, each leaf 4-8 inches (10-20 cm) long, rough-textured and rounded or heart-shaped at the base. Found between 3,500-7,000 feet elevation in the mountains of the West, blooming from late June to August. It often comes in and takes over an area that has been overgrazed..

Common Pearly Everlasting, *Anaphalis margaritacea,* is truly a common plant for it is found over much of the United States, south from Alaska to Newfoundland. It is unusual because the dozens of round flower heads appear white with small yellow or brown centers. This is because the flowers are just tiny disc flowers and the many bracts of the bulging involucre are shiny, white, and papery, even in bud. As the flowers mature, they too become white and soft-fuzzy, the bracts spread out and the whole flower stalk dries and is more or less "everlasting."

Ten to fifteen flower heads grow in a cluster, with many such clusters grouped together at the top of each 1-3 foot (30-90 cm) leafy white stem. The alternate leaves are long and narrow, 4 inches (10 cm) at the base to 1 inch (2.5 cm) at stem top. The underside is very gray and woolly. Many stems grow from a perennial base. If you examine the flower heads with a magnifying glass, you find mostly heads with just tiny pistillate flowers (with perhaps a few staminate flowwers in the center). Other plants will

DANDELION

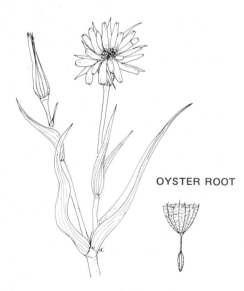

OYSTER ROOT

produce just staminate flowers (of course, producing no seeds). The minute corolla of the pistillate flower is thread-like, the style extending beyond it. Blooms from June to August, depending on altitude and habitat, the head persisting in dried form long into the fall and early winter.

3. DANDELION-LIKE: RAY FLOWERS ONLY

This group of Composites have heads with ray flowers only. The member known to almost everyone everywhere is the dandelion. This group is large, with members all over the world. Most of the plants have milky, bitter juice and leaves are mostly basal. The flower stalks are hollow, usually leafless, with a single head of flowers at the top. The flowers are on a naked flat receptacle.

Dandelion, *Taraxacum vulgare,* is a garden weed all over the world, producing several flowering stems from basal leaves. The blossoms last only one day, then mature into a head of fluffy white pappus which scatters the seeds with the wind. The leaves of this plant, if young and succulent, are excellent for greens, salads, or fried. The dried roots are made into a drug, taraxacum. Roots also can be roasted till dark brown and ground to make a coffee substitute. In Russia, the milky juice is a commercial source of rubber; the United States experimented with this source of rubber during World War II. The common name of dandelion comes from the French *dent-de-lion* meaning "lion's tooth." It gets this name from the toothlike lobes of the leaf edge.

False Dandelion, Goat Chicory, *Agoseris vulgare (glauca),* looks like a tall dandelion with its flat head of yellow rayflowers. The hollow leafless flower stalk from basal toothed leaves is 4-25 inches (10-60 cm) tall, bearing a single flower head 1-2 inches (2.5-5 cm) across. The main difference is that the achene is smooth while the true dandelion has finely spined achenes; also the flower is a lighter, softer yellow color. The flower structure resembles chicory, but that plant grows very differently. This species, and its varieties, is found abundantly in meadows, alongside roads, on slopes at almost all elevations all over the West, usually blooming three to four weeks later than dandelions. Blooms May-August, depending on elevations. *Agoseris aurantiaca* is a closely related species found only in the higher elevations in the mountains of the West, and is deep orange or rusty-brown in color. A similar lovely orange dandelion is found in the alpine meadows of Europe.

Oyster Plant, Salsify, Goat's Beard, Jerusalem Star, *Tragopogon porrifolius,* is best known by its very large tan or brown seed head 3 inches (7.5 cm) or more across. It looks like a huge brown dandelion head, each "seed" having a parachute of fine pappus hairs attached to the achene. The flat deep purple heads of ray flowers are attractive and showy, growing at the tip of a 1-4 foot (30-120 cm) hollow stem. The outer ray flower corollas are much longer than those toward the center; each is five-toothed at the tip, and has both stamens and pistils. The head is

CHICORY

TACK STEM

surrounded by long slender bracts in one row, extending beyond the rays. These perennial herbs have milky juice, a thick taproot, and long clasping grass-like leaves. It was brought to America by the early colonists. The root makes a good vegetable, tasting somewhat like oysters or parsnips- —should be used before stalk flowers: Scrape, slice and cook like carrots. This species is cultivated in some areas for its root. The milky juice was coagulated and used by the Indians to chew like gum. The flower opens in the morning, usually closing by noon, and wilting quickly if picked. As the seeds mature, the head reopens as a big fluffy ball. Oyster plant grows along moist valley roadsides from low elevations to 7,000 feet over much of the West, and also in the East. Bloom May to July, with seed heads seen everywhere in August. *Tragopogon dubius* is a yellow species, often found with the purple species. The bracts around the flower head are much longer than the ray flowers.

Chicory, *Cichorium intybus,* is a perennial from Europe which has made itself at home all over America. It has large basal leaves, slender, hairy stems, and a milky, bitter juice. The heads of ray flowers are scattered along the almost leafless stem. Some of the varieties have flowers which are pink or yellow, but the most common variety has dainty, beautiful blossoms of a lovely, unmistakeable shade of china blue, making a colorful accent against dried grass and weeds. Each ray is five-toothed at the tip and ½-1 inch (1.3-2.5 cm) long. The receptacle is flat, usually with chaff-like bracts or bristles.

Chicory has a deep taproot which some Europeans roast and grind to use instead of coffee, or to mix with coffee. It is a close relative of the endive which we use in salads, and a distant relative of oyster plant, which also has been used as food. Chicory blooms late in the summer, along roadsides and in fields, all over America.

Tack Stem, *Calycoseris wrightii, Calycoseris parryi,* is one of the beautiful desert annuals found from western Texas to Utah, and throughout the southwestern deserts of New Mexico, Arizona, and California. On the flowering branches are many noticeable small glands which appear like tacks stuck lightly into the stem. The flowers are typical of this group of ray-flowers-only, each ray having five tiny notches at the tip. The notches are very noticeable in the white tack stem, *Calycoseris wrightii,* the ray flowers becoming pink on the underside. The tacks are yellowish and the stems may be pinkish at the base. The yellow tack stem, *Calycoseris parryi,* has yellow, shorter ray flowers with dark tacks on the upper stems and the leaves are smaller. The plants are much branched, growing 4-12 inches (10-30 cm) high, with most of the deeply divided leaves forming a basal clump. Common on rocky slopes, mesas, and open areas 1,200-4,000 feet elevation, appearing as soon as enough winter moisture has come, and blooming by early spring. The blossom is very similar to that of chicory.

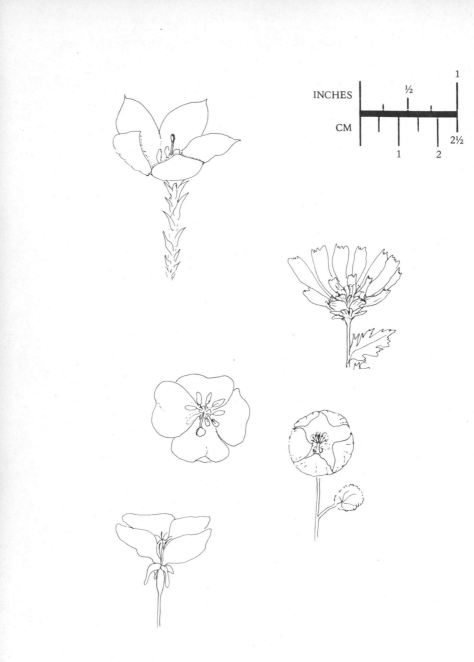

INCHES

½

1

CM

1

2

2½

BELLY FLOWERS

190

Chapter XII

BELLY FLOWERS

To see the miniatures of the plant world, you must "get down on your belly." Get the view that an insect or even a worm has of the flowers in the "Grassroots Jungle." Look eye-to-eye with a tiny plant and see its wonderful flower.

Where do you find them? Most anywhere: city, country, mountain, coast, desert. The vacant lot next door or that crevice in the broken pavement or sidewalk, your lawn, the playground, the soccer field, the golf courses are all places in populated areas where you can find fascinating belly flowers. There are many conditions or factors that produce or influence a city belly flower population. Lots of traffic, too little water, too much heat, too much smog, too little chance to grow big (even including the lawn mower that would chop off anything that got very tall). And there's the windy beach, the dry desert, the alpine mountain areas all with their belly flower populations.

The desert, of course, is often a vast belly flower wild garden. There may be hundreds of different kinds of flowers in one small area. But to see them you have to really get down. Photographers often set a dime beside plants to show relative size, and the flowers are often smaller! The low rainfall is the main factor here. When the rain comes, the seeds germinate, the plant grows, perhaps with only a leaf or two, the flower blooms, and quickly matures its seeds. All of this in rapid succession while the plant has enough water to function. The growing period is too short to produce tall stems and many or large leaves. Desert flowers are marvelous energy conservationists; they make do with unbelievably little water. In wet years, they may produce many small flowers; in drier years, just a few with only a leaf or two, but they still bloom and produce their seeds.

Temperature is probably the main factor in high mountain areas; by the time the deep snows have melted in many high areas, it is late, late summer. The plant has only a little time to grow and reproduce before cooler weather and frosts of fall will slow down or put an end to the growing season.

A lawn or park or playing field is constantly having the grass mowed, so if flowers succeed there, the leaves and blossoms must be short enough not to be mowed. Plants may have wide spreading stems, often making a mat which produces low flowers, or they may be in tiny low clumps. Rangelands that are constantly "mowed" by cattle or sheep or deer have large populations of belly flowers; only those that could successfully miniaturize themselves (or at least keep their upper growth close to the ground) could produce their flowers which produce the seeds which would keep up the population.

But all of these flowers are worth "looking until you really see." A fun thing is to take just a little area, a square meter or two (throw out a hoola hoop) and see what you can find in just that space. How many kinds can you discover? Is each plant just tiny, or does it cover a large area sideways? Perhaps it has long flat branches or runners, yet stand only 1–3 inches (2½–8 cm) high. A dandelion in a lawn is a lovely example. The leaves are arranged as a rosette, radiating from the center, covering a large compact area for maximum exposure to light. The yellow flower seems to sit right down in the middle. However, as the flower withers and the developing seeds mature, the stem lengthens till the seed heads stand where wind or an animal touching it will loosen the tufted seeds and off they will fly with the air currents (or the mower), but the mower doesn't cut the low flower (where the seeds are only developing).

Look at the flowers with a magnifying glass. These miniatures become works of beauty and art, perfect in minute details. You can even count their parts. The sepals may be very reduced, the petals often tiny, but even the stamens and the pistil can be found. And most of them will be "keyable." The Pea Family has many belly flowers. Look for the characteristic larger upper petal (it is often folded over the others), two side petals and the tiny boat-shaped, practically stuck-together, bottom petals. Clovers are examples: Each head is a group of tiny pea flowers clustered at the end of a short stem. Many of the Composites are belly flowers. See if you can find tiny daisies, with minute ray and disc flowers, or dandelion relatives with just ray flowers. Some of the wild Geraniums (filaree) produce beautiful symmetrical leaf rosettes and tiny five-petaled flowers, with all the parts for you to find (with a magnifying glass). There are many tiny mints (square stems) and flowers belonging to the Mustard (four petals, six stamens) and Evening Primrose (four petals, eight stamens, inferior ovary). Of course, anything called a "ground cover" is really a belly flower. Look for their flowers.

Start looking for belly flowers—you'll be startled how many you find. A young soccer player once remarked that his attention was distracted the day after a belly flower field trip. He kept noticing the number and variety of the belly flowers on the playing field!

GLOSSARY

Achene: Small, dry, one-seeded fruit which doesn't break open.
Alternate: First on one side, then on the other.
Annual: Growing anew from seed each year.
Anther: The part of the stamen that produces pollen.
Axil: The angle between leaf and stem.
Biennial: Not blooming until the second year.
Blade: The flat, expanded part of the leaf or petal.
Bract: Modified or small-size leaf of a flower cluster.
Bulb: Cluster of fleshy storage leaves underground.
Calyx: The circle of sepals in a flower, all of them together.
Complete: Possessing sepals, petals, stamens, and pistils.
Corm: A thickened underground, solid fleshy stem base, as in Brodiaeas, Gladiola.
Corolla: The circle of petals in a flower, all of them together.
Claw: The narrow base of a petal.
Dicot: Plant with two seed leaves; netted veins.
Entire: Margin (of leaf) not toothed or notched.
Filament: Stem supporting the anther in a stamen.
Genus: A plant group made up of different species; the first part of the plant's scientific name; plural: *Genera*.
Herb: A plant without woody parts above ground; annual or perennial.
Hypanthium: A cup-shaped enlarged receptacle, enclosing the seeds when mature; especially found in the Rose Family.
Imperfect: Stamens in one flower or plant; pistil in another flower or plant.
Inferior Ovary: Ovary low in the flower with petals and calyx lobes *above* it.
Involucre: A circle of bracts surrounding a flower cluster, as around the head in the Sunflower (Composite) Family.
Leaflets: A division of a leaf of many parts, i.e. a division of a compound leaf.
Legume: A type of seed pod which opens on each side into two parts, as in Peas.
Lobe: The divisions of a united corolla, or of a leaf.
Monocot: Plant having only one seed leaf; parallel veins.

Nectar Gland: Tissues specialized to produce nectar.

Opposite: Located at same spot on stem across from each other (as opposite leaves); stamen stands in *front* of petal, not alternating with petal.

Palmately compound: Leaflets arranged like palm of a hand, all beginning at a common center.

Pappus: Modified calyx of Composites, usually papery, hairy, scaly, etc.

Peduncle: Stem of a flower or flower cluster.

Perennial: Living more than one year.

Perfect: A flower having both stamens and pistil in the *same* flower.

Petiole: The stalk (stem) or a *leaf.*

Pinnately compound: Leaflets arranged on each side of the leaf stem.

Pistil: The female, or seed-producing part of the flower; includes the stigma, the style, and the ovary.

Pistillate: Referring to a flower or plant having only flowers with pistils but no stamens.

Pollination: The process of pollen going from the stamens to the pistil.

Pome: Fleshy fruit from two- or more-parted ovary.

Prostrate: Not erect; lying more or less flat.

Raceme: Flowers in an elongated cluster along a single stalk, youngest flower at the top.

Receptacle: Enlarged part of stem where flower parts attach.

Regular: The parts having same size or shape.

Rootstalk: Underground root-like stem, growing roots on one side, shoots on the other.

Rosette: Group of leaves spreading in a circle.

Saprophyte: Living on decaying vegetation; contains no chlorophyll.

Sepal: One part or division of the calyx; outer flower "circle," protects flower in bud stage.

Sessile: Sits on something with no petiole or stem (as a sessile leaf).

Spike: Flowers with no stems (peduncles), each flower tightly attached to stalk.

Stamen: The male or pollen-producing organ of flower; includes anther and filament.

Staminate: Referring to a flower or plant producing flowers with stamens but no pistils.

Staminoidea: Stamens which do not produce pollen.

Sterile: Having no stamens or pistils; often true of ray flowers.

Stigma: Portion of the pistil that receives pollen.

Style: Slender part of pistil between ovary and stigma.

Succulent: Juicy.

Superior ovary: Ovary stands above attachment of petals, sepals and stamens.

Tendril: A slender climbing stem portion.

Umbel: Branches reaching same height and growing from same point; may refer to leaves, flowers, or flower clusters.

BIBLIOGRAPHY

Abrams, LeRoy. *Illustrated Flora of the Pacific States*. Stanford, California: Stanford University Press. Vol. 1, 1940; Vol. 2, 1944; Vol. 3, 1951; Vol. 4 by Roxana Ferris, 1960.

Angier, Bradford. *Feasting Free on Wild Edibles*. Harrisburg, Pa.: Stackpole Books, 1972.

Archibald, David, et. al. *Quick-Key Guide to Wildflowers*. Garden City, New York: Doubleday, 1968.

Armstrong, Margaret. *Field Book of Western Wildflowers*. New York: G. P. Putnam's Sons, 1915. Re-issued.

Arnberger, Leslie P. *Flowers of the Southwest Mountains*, 4th ed. Santa Fe, N.M.: Southwestern Monuments Assoc., 1968.

Balls, Edward K. *Early Uses of California Plants*. Berkeley: University of California Press, 1962.

Clements, Edith. *Flowers of Coast and Sierra*. Riverside, N.J.: Hafner Press, 1959 (orig. pub. 1928).

_____ *Rocky Mountain Flowers*, 3rd ed. Riverside, N.J.: Hafner Press, 1963 (orig. pub. 1928).

_____ *Flowers of Mountain and Plain*, 3rd ed. Riverside, N.J.: Hafner Press, 1955 (orig. pub. 1926).

_____ *National Geographic*, "Wild Flowers of the West." May 1927, pp. 566.

Craighead, John J. and Ray J. Davis. *Field Guide to Rocky Mountain Wildflowers*. Boston: Houghton Mifflin, 1963.

Dana, Frances T. *How to Know the Wildflowers*, rev. ed. N.Y.: Dover, 1963.

Delisle, Harold F. *Common Plants of the Southern California Mountains*. Healdsburg, California: Naturegraph, 1962.

Dodge, Natt N., and Jeanne R. Janish. *Flowers of the Southwest Deserts*, 8th ed. Sante Fe, N.M.: Southwestern Monuments Assn., 1973.

Ferris, Roxana S. *Death Valley Wildflowers*. Death Valley Nat. Hist. Assn., 1962.

_____ *Flowers of the Point Reyes National Seashore*. Berkeley: University of California Press, 1970.

Geary, Ida. *The Leaf Book;* Field Guide to Plants of Northern California. Fairfax, California: A. Philpott, 1972.

Gibbons, Euell. *Stalking the Wild Asparagus*. New York: David McKay Co., Inc., 1970.

Gilkey, H. M. *Handbook of Northwest Plants*. Portland, Oregon: Oregon State Univ. Bookstores, 1973.

Grimm, William C. *Recognizing Flowering Wild Plants*. Harrisburg, Pa.: Stackpole Books, 1968.

Harrington, Harold David, and L. W. Durrell. *How to Identify Plants*. Chicago: Swallow Press.

Haskin, L. L. *Wild Flowers of the Pacific Coast*, 2nd ed. Portland, Oregon: Binfords & Mort, 1970.

Hitchcock, Charles Leo, and Arthur Cronquist. *Flora of the Pacific Northwest*. Seattle: University of Washington Press, 1973.

House, Homer D. *Wildflowers*. New York: Macmillan, 1974.

Hull, Helen S. *Wildflowers for your Garden*. New York: M. Barrows & Co., 1952.

Hylander, Clarence J. *Flowers of Field and Forest*. New York: Mcmillan, 1962.

Jaeger, Edmund C. *Desert Wild Flowers*. rev. ed. Stanford, California: Stanford University Press, 1968.

Jepson, Willis Linn. *A Manual of the Flowering Plants of California*, rev. ed. Berkeley: University of California Press, 1960.

Kieran, John. *Introduction to Wild Flowers*. Garden City, N.Y.: Doubleday, 3rd ed.

Kingsbury, John Merriam. *Poisonous Plants of the United States and Canada*, 3rd ed. Englewood Cliffs, N.J.: Prentice-Hall, 1964.

Lemmon, Robert, and Charles C. Johnson. *Wildflowers of North America in Full Color*. Garden City, N.Y.: Doubleday & Co., 1961.

Lenz, Lee W. *Native Plants for California Gardens*. Claremont, California, Rancho Santa Ana Botanic Garden, 1956.

McDougall, W. B. and Herma A. Baggley. *The Plants of Yellowstone National Park*. Yellowstone Interpretive Series #8. Yellowstone Library and Museum Assn., Yellowstone Park, Montana 1956.

Mathews, F. Schuy Cir. *Field Book of American Wildflowers*. New York: Putnam's Sons, 1966.

Munz, Philip A., and David D. Keck. *A California Flora and Supplement*. Berkeley, University of California Press, 1973.

———*California Spring Wildflowers*. Berkeley: University of California Press, 1961.

———*California Desert Wildflowers*. Berkeley: University of California Press, 1962.

———*California Mountain Wildflowers*. Berkeley: University of California Press, 1963.

———*A Flora of Southern California*. Berkeley: University of California Press, 1974.

———*Shore Wildflowers of California, Oregon, and Washington*. Berkeley: University of California Press, 1965.

Niehaus, Theodore F. *Sierra Wildflowers: Mt. Lassen to Kern Canyon*. Berkeley: University of California Press, 1974.

Parsons, Mary Elizabeth. *The Wild Flowers of California*, 3rd ed. New York: Dover Pub., 1966.

Patraw, Pauline M., and Jeanne Janish. *Flowers of the Southwest Mesas*, 5th ed. Sante Fe, N.M.: Southwestern Monuments Assn., 1970.

Reisigl, Herbert, et. al. *The World of Flowers*. New York: Viking Press, 1966.

Rickett, Harold William. *Wildflowers of the United States*. 6 Volumes in 14 parts. New York: Botanical Garden, McGraw-Hill, 1966. Vol. 1, Northeastern States; Vol. 2, Southeastern States; Vol. 3, Texas; Vol. 4, Southwestern states; Vol. 5, Northwestern states, Vol. 6, Central Mountains and Plains.

Sharpe, G. and Wewonah Sharpe. *Wildflowers of Mt. Rainier National Park*. Seattle: University of Washington Press, 1957.

Sharsmith, Helen K. *Spring Wildflowers of the San Francisco Bay Region*. Berkeley: University of California Press, 1965.

Shumacher, Genny, et al. *The Mammoth Lakes Sierra*, 3rd ed. Berkeley: Wilderness Press, 1969.

Sweet, Muriel. *Common Edible and Useful Plants of the West*. Healdsburg, Ca.: Naturegraph, 1962.

Thomas, John Hunter. *Flora of the Santa Cruz Mountains of California*. Stanford, California: Stanford University Press, 1961.

Watts, Mary T. *Flower Finder*, Berkeley: Nature Study Guild, 1955.

INDEX

198 WILDFLOWERS OF THE WEST